Essential Tips for Woodturners

Essential Tips for Woodturners

Guild of Master Craftsman Publications Ltd

This collection first published in 1997 by
Guild of Master Craftsman Publications Ltd,
Castle Place, 166 High Street, Lewes,
East Sussex BN7 1XU

© GMC Publications 1997

ISBN 1 86108 054 9

Front cover photograph by Anthony Bailey
Illustrations by Simon Rodway

Designed by Derek Lee

Printed and bound in Great Britain
by Ebenezer Baylis & Son Ltd

CONTENTS

INTRODUCTION 1

SECTION 1

CHUCKS

CHEAP FACEPLATES 3

SCREWCHUCK FACEPLATE 4

NAPKIN RINGS FROM OFFCUTS 4

DOWEL HOLDER 6

SMALL DIAMETER SPLIT RING CHUCK 6

EXTENDED BOBBIN DRIVE 7

CHUCK WITH A DIFFERENCE 7

HOT-MELT GLUE CHUCK 8

A HOME-MADE CHUCK FOR A LATHE 9

SECTION 2

MODIFYING AND IMPROVING LATHES

'FIDDLE' FIXED 11

CHUCK LOCK BRACKET 11

MOBILE LATHE STAND 12

SIMPLE AND CHEAP DIVISION PLATE 13

CUTTING LATHE NOISE AND VIBRATIONS 14

QUICK RELEASE LEVERS FOR A RECORD DML 15

CUT-OUT SWITCH FOR A LATHE 16

LATHE MODIFICATION 18

MODIFYING A CORONET TOOLREST 18

BIG IDEAS 19

MASKING TAPE CUTS BELT COVER NOISE 19

Section 3

JIGS

Drilling Jig 21

A Jig to Align Your Drill Bit 21

Endgrain Faceplate 22

Template for Tiles 23

Bowl Segment Cutting Jig 24

Safe and Sound 25

Ratchet Straps 25

Drill Handle 'Plug' 25

Add on Indexing 26

Clock This 27

Accurate Angles 27

Centre Finding 28

Section 4

TOOLS

Ferrule Punch 29

Spanner Extension 29

Tough Toolrest 30

Thread Chasers 30

Pinch Chuck Guard 31

A Device for Freeing Work from Faceplate 31

Inside Contour Sanding Device 32

Snappy Dresser is a Smooth Operator 32

Rug-making Tool Helps Gluing 33

Make Your Own Simple Depth Gauges 33

Tools Made from Scrap Planer Blades 34

Arm Support for the RS2000 System 34

Multi-point Drive Centre 35

Make Your Own Cone Centre 36

WOODTURNING

YOUR INVITATION TO SUBSCRIBE...
A very special offer!

As a woodturner you are missing so much if you are not already subscribing to *Woodturning* magazine.

Published 12 times a year, *Woodturning* introduces you to an exclusive club where you can look over the expert's shoulders and learn from them in a totally practical way.

With articles by talented, expert authors to advise and inspire you, *Woodturning* is tailored to every level of skill and experience.

EVERY ISSUE BRINGS YOU

- Test reports to help select the right tools and equipment
- Technical articles to improve your skills
- The latest developments from around the world to keep you up to date
- Projects to enjoy whatever your level of skill and expertise

INTRODUCTORY OFFER

SAVE 20%...Subscribe today at this special rate and claim a FREE BOOK!

SECTION 5

TECHNIQUES

CLING FILM CONSERVES 37

TURNING BLANKS MADE FROM GLUED OFFCUTS 37

BUBBLE WRAP 38

THREAD CUTTING 38

PITH HARDENER 38

WOOD HARDENER 38

HOW TO MAKE A BLOCK PATTERN 39

CENTRING 40

QUICK DIVIDER SETTING 40

MAGIC FORMULA FOR TURNING BALLS 41

USE A RUBBER BALL AS A BUNG 42

STOCK PREPARATION 42

LONG HOLE BORING 43

LONG HOLE CLEANING 43

SHARP FINGERNAILS 44

SECTION 6

DUST EXTRACTION

PLASTIC TIPS 45

TOOL MOUNTING GANTRY 46

SHAVINGS REMOVAL FROM HOLLOW FORM 47

AN EASY WAY TO CLEAN-UP SHAVINGS 47

VACUUM CLEANING 48

ONE EXTRACTOR FOR SEVERAL MACHINES 49

DUST EXTRACTOR 50

VACUUM NOISE 50

VACUUM CLEANER DUST EXTRACTOR 51

DUST EXTRACTOR BUNG 52

EFFECTIVE DUST COLLECTOR 53

SECTION 7

SAFETY AND PROTECTION

SAFETY SCREEN 55

DUST JACKETS 56

FIRE EXTINGUISHERS 56

STANDBY BATTERY FOR A RACAL AIRHOOD 56

CLEANING EYE GEAR 57

VISOR PROTECTOR 57

SECTION 8

SANDING AND FINISHING

POLISHING STICK 59

SAFER SANDING, WITH STYROFOAM 59

SANDER CLEANING 60

MAKE DISC-CHANGING CHILD'S PLAY 60

SANDING WITH SOLE 60

SECTION 9

STORAGE

HIGH HOSE 61

BUD VASE FILLINGS 61

SIMPLE STORAGE 61

GARAGE STORAGE 61

HANDY TOOL CARRIER 61

TIDY SANDPAPERS 62

MIX CONTAINERS 62

BRUSH CLEANER 62

BRUSH SAVER 63

ABRASIVES HOLDER 63

AIRTIGHT SEAL 64

USE WINE BLADDERS FOR STORAGE 64

INDEX 66

INTRODUCTION

Woodworking is a lifelong learning experience. Two adages are equally applicable to the craft: 'You're never too old to learn' and 'You learn something new every day'. The tips which readers send in to *Woodturning* are excellent examples of just how apt they are.

These tips can be new ideas, old ideas re-assessed and improved, or improvisations and lash-ups. All are equally relevant.

Few woodworkers are rich enough to indulge their fancies, but most are ingenious and all are practical. The tips that fill this book are the natural result of this combination – lack of funds, as well as necessity, being the mother of invention.

Other than ingenuity, these tips and ideas demonstrate the willingness of woodworkers to exchange ideas. There is little talk of trade secrets, but a generous interchange, usually leading to more ideas and improvements. It helps that woodturners are 'gadget happy' and love to get new bits of kit to help production.

Despite the fact that wood is man's oldest craft material, with a longer history than any other, the tips here prove we are still finding out new ways of using it. There is always something new for us all to learn from each other.

I hope you find some of the ideas here useful.

Neil Bell, Managing Editor
Woodcarving *and* Woodturning *magazines*

SECTION 1
CHUCKS

CHEAP FACEPLATES

Faceplates can be made cheaply and easily by using brass pipe fittings which have a male thread at one end and a female at the other.

.The female thread goes on to the lathe, and a hole is bored into a thick ply disc to screw tightly on to the male thread.

A screw hole drilled into the edge of the disc and through the wall of the fitting, takes a deeply countersunk steel

screw which will resist any tendency for the threads in the ply to strip.

Mounted on the lathe and glued up, it can be used as a conventional faceplate or a glue chuck. If you know a friendly plumber who will give you some old fittings, the cost is negligible.

P.A. Symonds

Faceplate

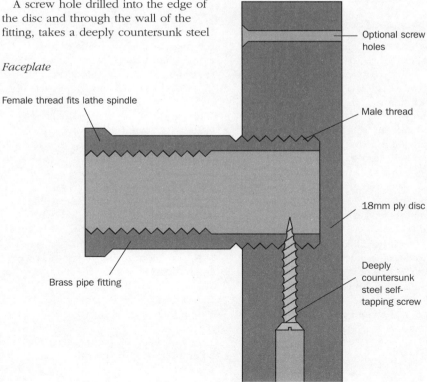

Female thread fits lathe spindle

Optional screw holes

Male thread

18mm ply disc

Brass pipe fitting

Deeply countersunk steel self-tapping screw

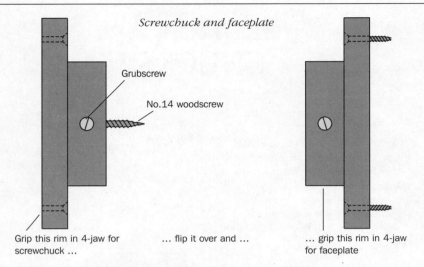

Screwchuck and faceplate

Grubscrew

No.14 woodscrew

Grip this rim in 4-jaw for screwchuck ...

... flip it over and ...

... grip this rim in 4-jaw for faceplate

SCREWCHUCK FACEPLATE

I have a Myford ML8 with a compound slide attachment for turning metal. Although the slowest lathe speed is 750RPM, which is a little fast, by using TCT cutting tools I can get a good finish.

To make my screwchuck I used a 25mm, 1" thick disc 90mm, 3½" dia.

Gripped in my Axminster four-jaw chuck, I trued one face and about 10mm, ⅜" of the edge, to about 85mm, 3⅜" DIA. I then reversed the workpiece to true the second face, and reduce about 15mm, ⅝" to 50mm, 2" dia.

A central hole takes a No.14 38mm, 1½" woodscrew, held in place by a grub screw. To mount it on the lathe I hold it in the four-jaw chuck on the larger rim.

After a while I realised that holes drilled in the large disc gave me a small faceplate.

Neil Poston

NAPKIN RINGS FROM OFFCUTS

Looking through my hardwood store, I found I had a lot of offcuts, mainly of about 50mm, 2" diameter. I decided to turn them into napkin rings, in sets of six.

It was simple to drill and enlarge the inside of the rings and to make them 35mm, 1⅜" long. The problem was how to hold the hollow rings so I could turn the outside.

This cannot be done with an expanding chuck without damaging the inner surface. So I developed the hardwood ring holder shown. It consists of five parts.

1. A long piece fits in my chuck, with a tapered end which has a central hole for a dowel.

2. A dowel provides stability, being a sliding fit in the holes in the tapered pieces.

3. A short tailstock piece with similar taper and dowel hole as the long section.

4 & 5. Two expanding pieces grip the work.

The gripping pieces are turned in one piece, as a ring with internal tapers, then cut in two lengthways. Saw cuts about 3mm, ⅛" apart, are made in both ends of the gripping pieces, so that as they expand in a napkin ring they distort to give a better grip.

In use, the long piece is held in the chuck, the dowel inserted, and the short piece goes on the dowel. The gripping pieces sit either side of the dowel and a napkin ring slides over them.

The tailstock is brought up, and as pressure is applied the gripping pieces are forced out to hold the ring. More tailstock pressure increases the grip.

I can complete the turning, sand and polish the outside of napkin rings on this holder.

I also use a split ring to hold the napkin rings, so I can finish inside them.

Mr & Mrs F Bridge

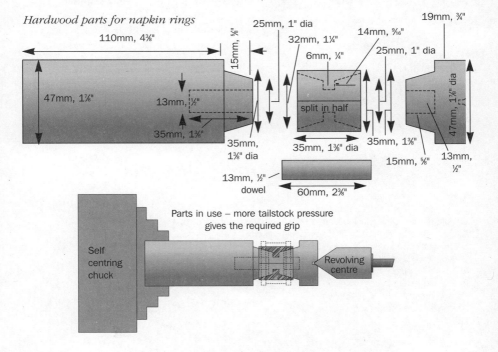

Hardwood parts for napkin rings

Parts in use – more tailstock pressure gives the required grip

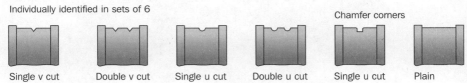

Individually identified in sets of 6

Chamfer corners

Single v cut   Double v cut   Single u cut   Double u cut   Single u cut   Plain

DOWEL HOLDER

I had to turn some small pieces out of dowels. To hold them I made a wooden centre to fit my hollow lathe spindle and made three cuts in the end. This makes an excellent wooden collet chuck.

Place the dowel in the chuck and tap it lightly. Knock out the colleted work from the outboard end of the hollow spindle.

Lloyd Humiston

Taper to match that of lathe. Hole drilled to provide tightish fit for dowel, but not too tight

Dowel holder

Three sawcuts are made in the face of the taper collet chuck

SMALL DIAMETER SPLIT RING CHUCK

I wanted to turn needle boxes from some 30mm, 1⅛" x 32mm, 1¼" square lengths of hardwood. I decided to use a Craft Supplies precision combination chuck, but the size I had was too large.

In the end, I made up my own split ring chuck from beech. I screwed a piece of about 75mm, 3" dia to a wooden faceplate and turned to the dimensions shown.

If G in FIG 1 is too big, the ring fouls the threads when being removed. Otherwise it's not critical. The groove for

Small diameter split ring chuck

A. Cross section of split ring.
B. Cylindrical block to fill chuck body.
C. Hole left by screw chuck accommodates knib left on under cutting.
D. This diameter is a sliding fit to centralise the ring.
E. The slot in the workpiece should be slightly under 20mm ¾" and slightly over 6mm ¼" wide.
F. Groove for elastic band.
G. This diameter is very sloppy, to facilitate removal.

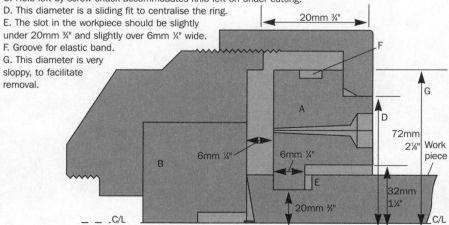

the rubber band holds the ring together when it has been cut in half and is being assembled on the workpiece.

I turned the workpiece to a cylinder using conventional four-prong drives and a revolving tailcentre, undercutting the tailend, so that when it is in the split ring chuck it is parallel to the axis of the lathe.

The block B (FIG 1) provided a firm base for the workpiece to be pressed against. I made it a push fit to enable easy removal. I've made several needle cases using this system, which holds the workpiece very firmly.

Ray Ridley

Extended Bobbin Drive

As I don't have a lace bobbin drive I have made a square socket drive that is held in my Axminster four-jaw chuck.

The square drive comes from an accessory to a socket spanner set – the long extension. Normally the long extension is a stout steel bar about 150mm, 6" long, with a square tip and a matching square socket at the other end. These are available for ⅜" or ½" drive, with ⅜" and ½" square sockets respectively. I use the ½" version, as lace bobbin blanks fit neatly into the end.

I could have used a shorter extension bar, but I wanted to keep well clear of the knobbly bits that stick out on the four-jaw chuck. I cut the extension bar down to about 125mm, 5" long – the first 25mm, 1" is held in the chuck, leaving 100mm, 4" clearance between the wood and the good though knobbly chuck.

Socket spanner extension bars can be found in secondhand tool shops, street markets and car boot sales for less than

50p, which is a considerable saving on a commercially made bobbin drive.

C.R. Oakes

Chuck with a Difference

Most of you will have used or seen the chuck that operates on the expansion principle, which sometimes splits work when tightened. Here is an alternative collet chuck which can be made up to do the same job using the contraction or reduction principle, though you'll need an engineer's lathe to make it.

It's made from 50mm, 2" heavy duty steel pipe, the first piece being 40mm, 1⅝" long, to which is welded a washer with a hole in the middle.

The opposite end is bevelled at the lip on the inside surface, about 3mm, ⅛", and holes drilled through the centre of the side wall, centred between top and bottom.

A washer or plug is welded to a second length of pipe. The plug is tapped to suit the threads of the spindle on your lathe (which accounts for the need for the 12mm, ½" thickness to provide a stable mount).

The exterior of this second piece is turned down to fit inside the first length. You may need to turn the inside of the first length to allow the second length to fit.

It's drilled with 6mm, ¼" holes at 60° from the centre (six in all) and the walls are cut from the outer edge down to the centre of each 6mm, ¼" hole. This will permit the contraction required to hold the workpiece.

To use the chuck, the first section is placed over the lathe spindle and held while the second length is threaded on by hand to a snug fit. ➤

Walter Last's collet chuck

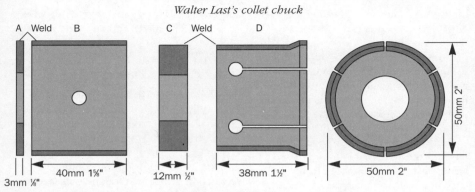

A Plate washer 3mm, ⅛" thick x 50mm, 2" dia. 22mm, ⅞" hole.   Weld to B
B 50mm, 2" HD steel pipe 40mm, 1⅝" long. 6mm, ¼" hole, 20mm, ¾" from bottom edge
C Steel disc 12mm, ½" thick x 50mm, 2" dia. with 20mm, ¾" hole tapped to suit. Weld to D
D Pipe 38mm, 1½" long turned as shown to fit inside B. Holes drilled at 60° centres and sawn from
   top to hole centre to permit contraction when tightened.

A wrench made from 12mm, ½" rod welded to a half circle of pipe about ½" wide with a 6mm, ¼" pin is welded to the outer end, to engage in the hole in the side wall of the first length.

The whole is turned clockwise with friction causing the second length to tighten and thus hold the work. The workpiece requires a centred circular ring cut in the bottom, of the same diameter as the chuck before contraction, and about 3mm, ⅛" deep. The chuck is inserted into this ring and the whole tightened as described above. It's pretty good for a home-made collet chuck.

Walter Last

HOT-MELT GLUE CHUCK

Glue sets quickly on hot-melt glue chucks, making it difficult to centre the workpiece. And when the work is parted off, the chuck gets smaller, so new ones have frequently to be made.

To solve this I made a hot-melt glue chuck with a wooden back and a thin aluminium faceplate.

I turned a piece of close-grained wood (19mm thick by 95mm diameter, ¾ x 3¾") with a dovetail recess to fit my Axminster Carlton Multichuck. The dimensions can be adjusted to suit any similar chuck.

Within the recess I drilled eight radial holes of 13mm, ½" diameter and a centre hole of 19mm, ¾".

I jigsawed a 119mm, 4¾" diameter circle from a 3mm, ⅛" thick aluminium plate, and drilled six countersunk holes around the circumference to take ½" brass screws.

I screwed the metal plate to the wooden block and mounted the new chuck on the lathe.

With a scraper, I trimmed the soft alloy disc round and scribed concentric lines into the face, to help centre work.

In use, the aluminium disc is heated with a hot air stripper and glue is applied with a hot melt glue gun. The retained heat in the metal plate keeps

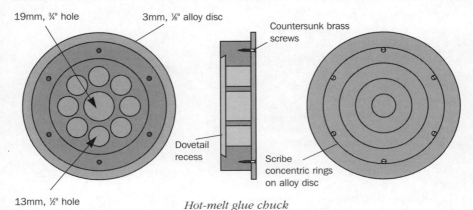

19mm, ¾" hole

3mm, ⅛" alloy disc

Countersunk brass screws

Dovetail recess

Scribe concentric rings on alloy disc

13mm, ½" hole

Hot-melt glue chuck

the glue plastic for some time, enabling the glue chuck to be centred at leisure.

When you've finished turning, the chuck can be easily removed by re-heating the disc through the holes in the back and around the rim.

While the glue is soft it can be scraped from the alloy disc, allowing the chuck to be used indefinitely.

H. Burton

A Home-made Chuck for a Lathe

When I first bought my lathe, I turned small items for pleasure. But as I turned my mind to bigger and better

woodturning projects, I realised that I needed a chuck.

I rushed out to buy one, but was stopped in my tracks by the price. Not to be deterred, I set about making my own.

I attached a piece of wood, a couple of inches in depth to the lathe's faceplate, and turned it to a cylinder with a diameter similar to that of the faceplate.

I turned a hole through the centre to create a ring of wood about 25mm, 1" or so wide. Four slivers were cut from the ring to create two pairs of parallel sides

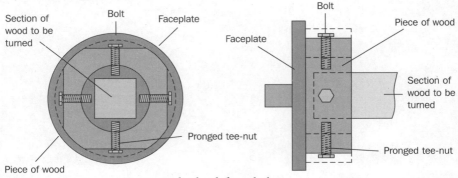

Section of wood to be turned

Bolt

Faceplate

Bolt

Piece of wood

Faceplate

Section of wood to be turned

Pronged tee-nut

Piece of wood

Pronged tee-nut

Home-made chuck for a lathe

at right angles to each other.

I drilled a hole in the middle of each of the straightened sides. Each hole was at right angles to the side it was going through and went all the way from the outside to the inside of the squared-off ring.

A pronged tee-nut was inserted in each hole, so the bolt could be screwed in, their ends protruding in the ring's inside.

One end of a section of wood to be turned is placed within the ring, the bolts tightened until the section of wood is held safely and securely and is ready to be turned.

It was easy to make – and quite cheap, though it's not self-centring.

Graham Watson

Section 2
MODIFYING AND IMPROVING LATHES

'Fiddle' Fixed

I found a big drawback to changing speeds on my Clarke CWL6B lathe was the 'fiddly' job of removing and replacing two small screws in the pulley housing door.

I solved this by doing away with the screws and fitting a 25mm, 1" piece of self-adhesive Velcro strip 25mm, 1" above each screw hole on the side of the machine, then another on the front, in line with the first.

I used a 50mm, 2" piece of Velcro, with the paper still left on the adhesive side, to join the side and front pieces, so making a safe and quick-to-use door fastener.

George Capon

'Fiddle' fixed

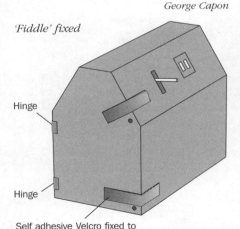

Hinge

Hinge

Self adhesive Velcro fixed to headstock and door

Chuck Lock Bracket

My Peter Child Master Chuck has a useful range of accessories, bar one – a third hand to prevent the chuck body rotating while I'm busy supporting the workpiece, tighting it in, or releasing it from the chuck.

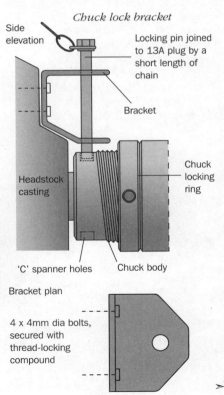

Chuck lock bracket

Side elevation

Locking pin joined to 13A plug by a short length of chain

Bracket

Chuck locking ring

Headstock casting

'C' spanner holes

Chuck body

Bracket plan

4 x 4mm dia bolts, secured with thread-locking compound

The lathe's index-lock is not the thing to abuse for this purpose.

My lathe has a vertical surface just above the headstock spindle, a short distance from the back of the chuck. So I was able to make a locking pin assembly strong enough to make the Masterchuck 'C' spanner redundant.

Using a 38 x 4mm, 1½ x ⅛" steel strip, I made a bracket, bent it to shape, and drilled and ground it to remove any sharp corners.

I fastened this to the headstock with four widely-spaced 4 x 12mm bolts to eliminate distortion. I drilled holes vertically through the bracket to accept a 5mm, ³⁄₁₆" tool-steel pin, which, when lowered through the bracket into the 'C' spanner hole in the chuck body, prevents the chuck rotating.

Before anyone, or my belt drive, protests at the safety implications of such an arrangement, I must add that the pin is attached to the lathe's 13A plug by a very short chain, so the plug must be removed from the socket, isolating the machine, before the drive can be locked.

Before making your chucklock, ensure it will not obstruct faceplates etc.

Bill Gilson

MOBILE LATHE STAND

I have a Myford ML8 lathe mounted on a robust wooden stand which includes a locker and cupboard for tools and accessories. The trouble is my workshop is only 12ft x 8ft, so to make the best use of the available space I have to be able to tuck the lathe out of the way when it is not in use.

As the lathe and its stand weigh about 120kg it is too heavy to move unaided. So I bought two car pillar jacks from a scrapyard for £2 each and modified them so the lathe can be raised onto heavy duty castors.

The jacks are permanently fixed to the lathe stand, so the operation of raising

Mobile lathe stand

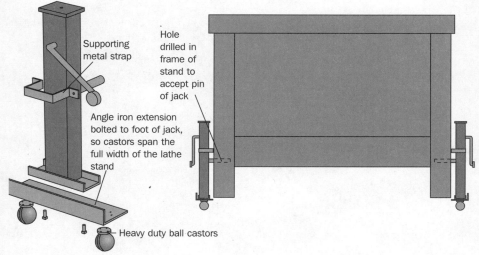

Supporting metal strap

Hole drilled in frame of stand to accept pin of jack

Angle iron extension bolted to foot of jack, so castors span the full width of the lathe stand

Heavy duty ball castors

or lowering takes only a few seconds. Once raised, the lathe can be moved by finger pressure, yet when lowered onto its stand is as solid as a rock.

D.E.G. Davies

SIMPLE AND CHEAP DIVISION PLATE

I made a cheap and easily-made division plate to take the place of a change wheel gear on the mandrel of an old Drummond round bed lathe.

It could also extend the range of indexing originally obtainable by mounting a standard change wheel gear on the mandrel to index the mandrel rotation.

The division plate is basically a bicycle chain, or similar, fitted to a wooden disc which is then mounted on the mandrel at the rear of the lathe headstock (FIG 1).

A spring index finger mounted at the back of the lathe engages with the chain to prevent rotation of the division plate in various positions (FIG 2).

To make the chain division plate, you first have to decide on the maximum number of divisions you want the unit to provide. The number chosen will need a length of chain with the number of links equal to the number of chosen divisions. For example, a 40-division plate will need a chain of 40 links (including the coupling link).

A normal coupling link with fish type spring clip can be used, but you may have to slightly modify the clamping disc to accommodate the extra thickness of this link.

I preferred to open up the holes in two link plates and make pointed pins that could be driven into the main body to make doubly sure the chain could not slip around (FIG 3).

Note that the division plate shown is bushed, to fit a Drummond lathe, but this can be modified to fit most types of lathe.

Derek C.K. Pearce

Simple and cheap division plate

FIG 1 Chain and disc

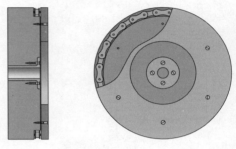

FIG 2 Spring index finger

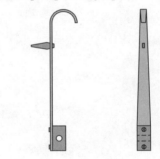

FIG 3 Pins to link chain plates

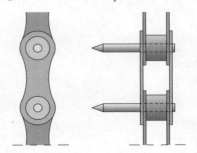

CUTTING LATHE NOISE AND VIBRATIONS

To reduce noise and vibration from a lathe mounted on a wooden floor I use a foam rubber mattress, 6'6" x 3' x 4", cut into four equal sections.

To make it, I sawed two pieces of 20mm, ¾" ply or blockboard to about 460mm, 18" x 760mm, 30", and then placed one section of foam rubber on another, with the plywood on top,

repeating this over the area where the lathe previously stood.

I set the wooden support trestle on both, and the lathe's weight against the trestle compressed the foam 'sandwiches' to about half the combined thickness.

Next, I made an L-shaped bracket, together with a wall mounting bracket and two double-ended rubber bushes taken from a defunct washing machine/spin drier.

Not to scale

Lathe dampening details

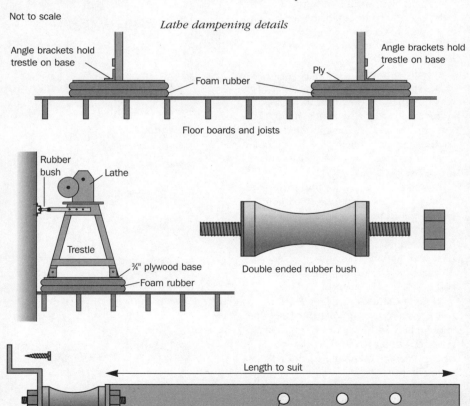

Angle brackets hold trestle on base

Foam rubber

Ply

Angle brackets hold trestle on base

Floor boards and joists

Rubber bush

Lathe

Trestle

¾" plywood base

Foam rubber

Double ended rubber bush

Length to suit

50mm 2"

6mm sprouting bolt or similar

Metal bracket

14

These were connected up and fastened to the wall behind the lathe and the trestle. I passed a 6mm bolt through the long leg of the L-bracket and trestle top, allowing some movement to compensate for settlement.

In use, I considered the noise to be cut by 90% and vibrations, or 'drumming', eliminated. The lathe exhibited no 'orbital' tendencies – what movement there was, was absorbed by the double layer of foam rubber.

The combined weight, together with stay bars, should keep everything safely earthbound – mine does.

As a matter of interest, my lathe was made by me to my own design, taking me three months to build in my spare time. Of substantial fabrication, it contains most features found in top of the range machines. It's the eighth lathe I have built over the years, each one an improvement on the last, and has served me well for three years.

I have turned blanks of 255mm x 150mm, 10" x 6" on a faceplate with no problems.

John Walton

Quick Release Levers for a Record DML

As a beginner at turning, I bought a Record DML24 lathe and have found it more than suitable for my needs so far. However it has been tedious continually searching for Allen keys and a spanner among the shavings, to adjust the toolrest and tailstock.

My first 'improvement' was to buy Allen keys from the local secondhand tool shop (cost 60p), cut them to suitable lengths and glue them into the grub screws. Scrap was then turned to make handles for the toolrest and tailstock barrel and a knob for the headstock guard.

The toolrest banjo, tailstock, and headstock bolts posed a bigger problem, as Record do not yet make quick release levers that fit the DML. Necessity was therefore again the mother of invention and another visit to the secondhand tool shop cost me £2 for two ¾" AF ring spanners and a 12mm x 100mm coach bolt (19mm ring spanners would be better but not so cheaply found).

The necessary modifications are shown in FIGS 1–3.

In the case of the tailstock, (FIG 1), the casing will not allow the bolt to be dropped through from the top, hence the need to glue the bolt head to the spanner and feed the bolt through from underneath as per the original arrangement.

Note the captivating lugs on the square straps need to be filed flush (FIG 2) and the upper faces of the nut and bolt head are fixed slightly proud of the spanner to avoid unnecessarily stressing the glue when tightening.

The ring spanners should be cranked no more than 20mm ¾", otherwise there is insufficient clearance from the bench to operate the levers comfortably. My tailstock lever is made from a straight spanner as shown and works perfectly.

The levers can be smartened up with car body filler and paint.

As the headstock is not so often moved, the modification shown simply makes access with the spanner easier. Having to fiddle about with a spanner inside the casing among pulleys and belts not only amounts to bad design but is potentially dangerous.

What about a bit of safety in design as ➤

Quick release levers for a Record DML

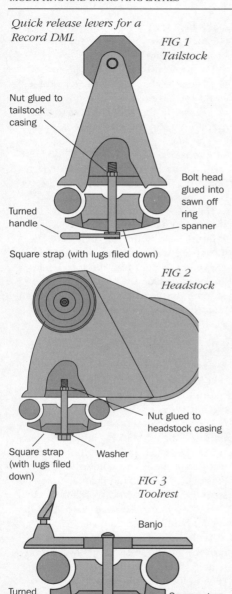

FIG 1
Tailstock

Nut glued to tailstock casing

Bolt head glued into sawn off ring spanner

Turned handle

Square strap (with lugs filed down)

FIG 2
Headstock

Nut glued to headstock casing

Square strap (with lugs filed down)

Washer

FIG 3
Toolrest

Banjo

Turned handle

Square strap (with lugs filed down)

Nut glued into sawn off ring spanner

per HSE recommendations!

If a lever is needed on the headstock, then a ratchet ring spanner will be necessary, as the end brackets supporting the bed prevent the rotation of a 'fixed' lever.

B.P. Holmes

CUT-OUT SWITCH FOR A LATHE

A handy device for turners is a cut-out switch for the lathe. This is simply a foot pedal made in the form of a narrow, flat-bottomed box with a hinged lid.

The lid rests on a spring-loaded press switch (taken from a vacuum cleaner), on the underside of which is glued coarse grained glasspaper or a thin rubber strip, to prevent it sliding about.

A hole is drilled in the hinge end of the box for the power cable to pass through to the switch, the current passing up the live (positive) wire and returning via the neutral (negative).

The strength/power rating of the switch I found adequate for my motor, there not being a factory stop/start fitted to it. I would assume there would be many other similar switches obtainable from various sources which could match anybody's lathe.

Most bought, manufactured machines, already have their own stop/start mechanisms, but there are still plenty of people who don't have this equipment and who may like to take advantage of a foot-operated switch.

John Walton

N.B. Readers are advised to ensure any reclaimed switch used is adequate to cope with the power rating of their lathe motor.

(See illustrations opposite.)

Foot-operated stop/start switch for a lathe

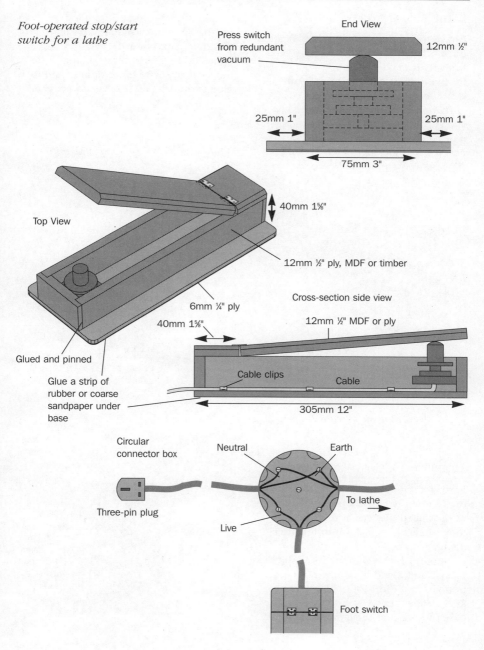

End View

Press switch from redundant vacuum

12mm ½"

25mm 1"   25mm 1"

75mm 3"

40mm 1⅝"

Top View

12mm ½" ply, MDF or timber

6mm ¼" ply

40mm 1⅝"

Cross-section side view

12mm ½" MDF or ply

Glued and pinned

Glue a strip of rubber or coarse sandpaper under base

Cable clips   Cable

305mm 12"

Circular connector box

Three-pin plug

Neutral   Earth

Live

To lathe

Foot switch

LATHE MODIFICATION

I have found the following modification for my Tyme Avon lathe useful (FIG 1). It involves making a bottom fixing plate for the toolrest, tailstock and centre steady from ½" mild steel plate.

This plate means the toolrest, tailstock and steady can easily be removed or replaced, without having to fully unscrew the locking handle. It simply slips between the lathe bed bars.

W.J. Pimlett

11mm ⁷⁄₁₆"

12mm ½"

38mm 1½"

35mm 1⅜"

100mm 4"

Lathe Modification

MODIFYING A CORONET TOOLREST

For some time, the clamping system on my Coronet No 1 lathe gave me trouble, as dust filled the gap in the cast iron toolrest clamp, causing it to function ineffectively.

I modified my clamp as shown in FIGS 1 and 2 and have had no more trouble, as the Bristol handle gives me a 100% clamp action every time. It's also easier to use and to clamp up tight.

Care must be taken in drilling the hole for the 8mm thread, due to drilling into the 2mm gap, but if the nut and bolt is tightened to give an easy sliding fit for the toolrest shaft before drilling and then glued with Loctite, there is no problem.

P.B. Sawyer

Modifying a Coronet toolrest clamp (Green model)

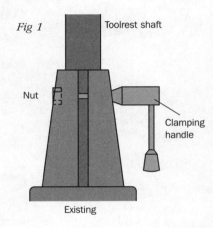

Fig 1

Toolrest shaft

Nut

Clamping handle

Existing

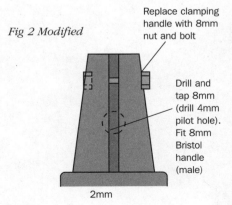

Fig 2 Modified

Replace clamping handle with 8mm nut and bolt

Drill and tap 8mm (drill 4mm pilot hole). Fit 8mm Bristol handle (male)

2mm

BIG IDEAS

I bought a second-hand Myford ML8 lathe, as it seemed sufficient for my needs. I soon found its limitations and decided to trade up to a Graduate.

It was easy to make the decision, but not so easy to find the money. As I saved for the new lathe I was faced with a choice, I could buy accessories for the Myford, but I would have to replace them when the Graduate arrived as they wouldn't fit both. Or, I could do without for now and buy them for the Graduate when I got it.

Rather than restrict my turning by doing without I got a local engineering firm to make me an adaptor. The internal thread fits the Myford and it has the same external thread as the Graduate spindle. There's also a No.3 Morse taper internally. The flange is drilled for a tommy bar, for unscrewing it.

I can now buy accessories, safe in the knowledge that they will fit my longed for Graduate. Of course, if I keep both lathes I still only need one set of accessories.

K. Smith

MASKING TAPE CUTS BELT COVER NOISE

I recently experienced some vibration on my lathe, a Coronet No. 1 (an excellent machine).

It is bolted down to a very solid bench and, while there was no movement in the main body of the lathe, I finally tracked it down.

On this model, the drive belt cover is a loose metal plate, which was rattling away and causing the noise.

My cure was to place two strips of masking tape at each end of the underside of the cover. Result – peace restored.

Tom Lack.

Spindle thread adaptor, Myford to Graduate

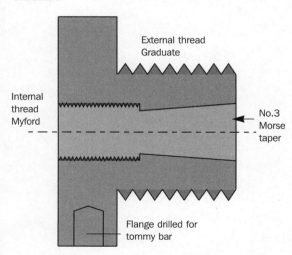

External thread Graduate

Internal thread Myford

No.3 Morse taper

Flange drilled for tommy bar

SECTION 3
JIGS

DRILLING JIG

This is my idea for a jig for drilling pen blanks and light pulls accurately. Initially I made it out of hardwood, then had it made in metal.

It is similar to a toolrest, but with a flat base and a perpendicular fence on one side.

To drill a pen blank, the centre of the blank is marked on the ends and the toolrest is replaced by the jig. With the drill in the headstock, the marked blank is held on the jig, which is positioned so that the blank is parallel to the lathe bed, the drill lined up with the centre mark on the end.

With the jig locked in position, the blank is pushed along the fence as the hole is drilled.

This arrangement is in excess of 90% accurate. The base and fence prevent squared blanks from twisting during drilling. The wooden version worked just as well as the metal one, I just wanted something durable for batch production work.

R.E. Vine

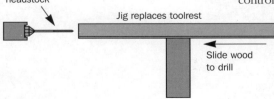

Drilling jig

25mm, 1"

254mm, 10"

64mm, 2½"

Stem to suit lathe

Drill bit in headstock

Jig replaces toolrest

Slide wood to drill

A JIG TO ALIGN YOUR DRILL BIT

I needed to drill holes into the perimeter of a turned disc for a recent project. I had an index plate, but no means of accurately aligning the drill bit, so I made the jig shown here.

It consists of a box which holds an electric drill, sliding on a base board, and held in place by rebated runners. An adjustable depth stop on one runner controls the depth of hole drilled.

The base of the drill box is made from melamine-faced chipboard, as this is smooth and slides easily. The rest are all offcuts of blockboard or hardwood, and the stem is turned to fit the toolrest banjo.➤

Tolerances need to be close to achieve accurately drilled holes, so a little grease may be needed to help things slide smoothly.

I worked my sizes out so that when the base plate is sitting on top of the banjo, the centre of the drill bit is on the centre line of the lathe. However, it does have adjustment upwards, just like a toolrest.

My jig is designed to be used in the toolrest banjo positioned on the 90° bowl turning attachment of my Thyme Avon lathe. It is not practicable to give measurements, as it all depends on the type of lathe and electric drill used.

It would, of course, be quite simple to make a bracket to fix to your bench or lathe stand.

Peter Symonds

ENDGRAIN FACEPLATE

Mounting the endgrain of wood on to a faceplate is a problem because screws hold badly. There is a real risk of the screws tearing out under side load.

I use the hole in the centre of the faceplate to overcome the problem. A spigot turned on the work fits in the unused part of the mounting thread in the faceplate.

My lathe is a Record DML24, which has a 19mm, ¾" spindle and a 100mm, 4" faceplate. I use a 1.6mm, ¹⁄₁₆" thick copper washer on the spindle to stop the faceplate locking in place.

When the faceplate is on the lathe there is a 9.5mm, ⅜" gap between the end of the spindle and the face of the faceplate. To utilise this, I first rough turn the blank between centres and square up both ends.

A jig to align your drill bit

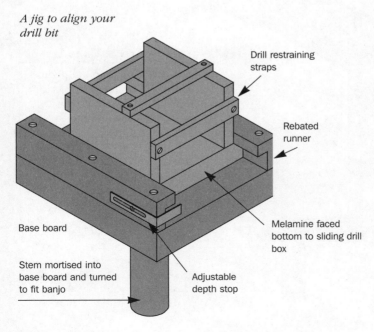

Drill restraining straps

Rebated runner

Melamine faced bottom to sliding drill box

Base board

Stem mortised into base board and turned to fit banjo

Adjustable depth stop

On one end I turn a 19mm, ¾" dia spigot 9.5mm, ⅜" long. I also slightly dish the face of this end for a firm seating on the faceplate.

Off the lathe, I screw the faceplate on to the spigot then use four woodscrews to reinforce the fixing. Blanks up to 150mm, 6" don't always need the woodscrews.

Back on the lathe, the tailstock is used for extra support while the outside is turned to a finish. The tailstock is removed for hollowing. The work is then parted off clear of the screws.

I loose no more than 19mm, ¾" of wood from the end, including the spigot. Should a longer spigot be thought prudent, a distance piece mounted on the faceplate can be used. Using this method I have turned vessels up to 300mm, 12" high and 150mm, 6" dia.

These measurements are for my Record lathe and 100mm, 4" faceplate. The spigot length and diameter will be different on other lathe and faceplate combinations.

N.S. Davies

TEMPLATE FOR TILES

Plywood templates are useful for fitting 150mm, 6" and 90mm, 3½" dia ceramic tiles into turned work.

For if you use a tile to check the recess and it becomes stuck in the workpiece, dislodging it can damage either the tile or the piece.

A ply disc is easier to. fit and remove and can be used to check the bottom for correct seating.

Use good quality birch ply discs, of exactly the same size and thickness of the tile. Drill a 10mm, ⅜" hole in the centre for easy removal and storage.

Tony Evans

Endgrain faceplate fixing

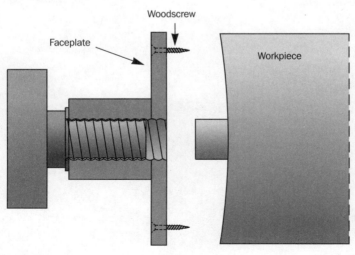

BOWL SEGMENT CUTTING JIG

I enjoy making bowl blanks from segments or staves, but originally found it difficult to hold small pieces of wood while cutting them on my radial arm saw, and also to set the arm to the exact angle.

As I wanted to cut segments of different sizes and angles, also staves, with parallel or tapered sides, the jig had to hold the pieces of wood at the correct angle and position while the radial saw arm was set at 90°.

The final design, in use replaces the radial arm fence and is clamped in place with the fence clamping system.

The jig's adjustable fence can be set at any angle so the component overhangs the side of the jig. The fence is locked in place with two 6mm, ¼" hexagonal nuts. The end stop can then be positioned against the component and locked in position.

The component clamps (one or two, according to the length of timber being cut) are placed over the side fence clamping bolts and locked in place by the wing nuts and washers.

When staves are being cut, the adjustable fence can be set parallel with the side face of the jig using an adjustable square, the radial arm saw blade being tilted to the correct angle and the end stop being reversed if necessary.

If tapered staves are required, the side fence can be set at the correct angle and proceed as above.

To aid in the setting of the side fence at regularly used angles, I made a series of triangular shaped templates out of 3mm, ⅛" thick plywood, taking care to mark each with both the included angle and the number of segments to make up a full circle.

John Webb

Bowl segment cutting jig

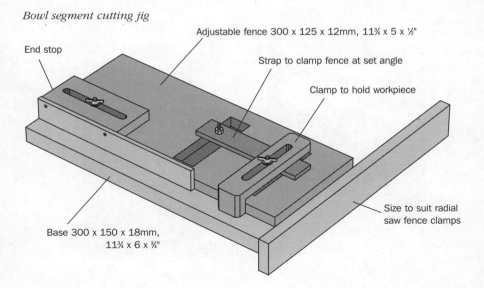

End stop

Adjustable fence 300 x 125 x 12mm, 11¾ x 5 x ½"

Strap to clamp fence at set angle

Clamp to hold workpiece

Size to suit radial saw fence clamps

Base 300 x 150 x 18mm, 11¾ x 6 x ¾"

SAFE AND SOUND

I came up with the following idea to overcome the problem of holding round timber securely without damage.

First I cut a piece of soft wood, about 25mm, 1" thick and the length of my vice jaws x 63mm, 2½" wide. Then I cut a V, as shown, leaving 20mm, ¾" in the centre.

To hold the wooden V to the vice jaw, I cut a piece of ⅟₁₆" sheet metal and bent it to fit the vice jaw, then fixed it with two wood screws.

It's also adaptable to a press drill vice, which I found very useful.

A. Taylor

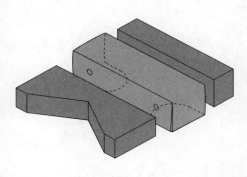

⅟₁₆" sheet metal

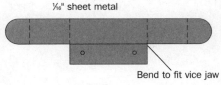

Bend to fit vice jaw

Safe and Sound

RATCHET STRAPS

One of the more irksome tasks is shaping awkward lumps of wood for faceplate turning. A useful method of doing this is to chainsaw it, and you can do this safely by tying the wood to a Workmate with a ratchet tie down strap, of the kind used for securing lorry loads.

The webbing is very strong (I carried out a 1,500lbs test on mine) and has a hook at each end which you attach to a strong part of the Workmate. Take up the slack and tension the strap using the ratchet buckle.

I bought my strap for a fiver at a weekly market, and it works like a charm. Stability is improved if the Workmate's jaws are wide open and if you cut on top of the table rather than over the end. Place scrap chipboard beneath the wood to protect the table.

Richard Pain

DRILL HANDLE 'PLUG'

I use an electric drill in a vice for rough grinding lathe tools with a 60 grit 5" Velcro 'flexidisc'.

The secret is to insert a tight 'plug' of wood into the hollow plastic side grip handle, so it can be gripped tightly and safely in the bench vice. Don't overload the handle by forcing the tool onto the disc.

This then enables you to set the drill horizontally, vertically, or at any angle. I know there are patent 'clamps' on the market, but most woodturners like to save money where they can.

When the sanding disc has reached the end of its useful life for wood, they are still quite effective for tool grinding jobs.

Tony Evans

ADD ON INDEXING

To make a spinning wheel and pomanders requested by my family I needed some means of accurately indexing, for drilling the spinning wheel hub and slit-sawing pomanders.

I had an old 360° metal protractor (plastic versions are available from drawing material stockists) which I mounted on an aluminium disc.

It's essential the disc is accurately marked. First mark a 20mm, ¾" central hole for the lathe nose spindle, then the diameter of the protractor (mine is 180mm, 7".) Mark four holes evenly spaced to fix the protractor to the backplate. I have given these ¹⁄₁₆" clearances on the external edge of the protractor to enable it to be rotated.

Drill and tap the holes 5mm (drill size 4.2mm). Then drill a central 12mm, ½"

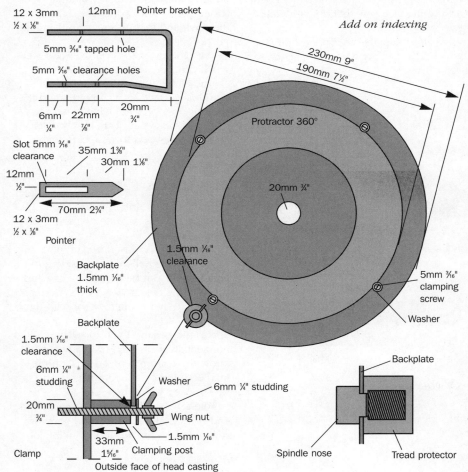

Add on indexing

hole and file this carefully to be a snug fit on the spindle nose shank.

I made a clamping post from a length of 20mm, ¾" bar measured from outside the face of the headcasting to the inside face of the backplate, minus ¹⁄₁₆" for clearance.

Drill through the centre and tap 6mm, ¼". Place the short piece of 6mm studding in one end and put on a washer and 6mm wing nut.

Clamp this on to the backplate, ensuring a ¹⁄₁₆" clearance between the studding and the edge of the backplate. Place in the position. Press gently against the headcasting and scribe round. Remove the post and from the scribed circle find the centre to drill and tap the headcasting 6mm, ¼".

Place a piece of 6mm, ¼" studding in the end of the clamping post to be screwed into the headcasting. Remove the backplate and protractor from the spindle nose, screw clamping the post into the headcasting, minus the wing nut and washer.

Replace the backplate and protractor on to the spindle nose, tighten, and check for clearance on the clamping post and studding. Replace the washer and wing nut.

Make a small bracket to mount the pointer on to the top centre of the headcasting. Make a slotted pointer to slide on the bracket.

Position the bracket on the centre line on top of the headcasting, mark holes, drill and tap headcasting 5mm, ³⁄₁₆".

The height of the bracket is determined by the size of the protractor used. Drill two holes in the top of bracket, drill and tap 5mm, ³⁄₁₆".

The workpiece can be placed in the lathe in the required position to start

drilling or marking. The backplate is then clamped in a fixed position with the wing nut.

Rotate the protractor to zero on the pointer, then tighten 5mm, ³⁄₁₆" screws around the protractor. Unclamping the backplate enables you to rotate the workpiece to any reading on the protractor.

This gadget can be used with faceplate, chuck and spindledrive, **but disconnect the power when it's fitted as it is like an un-guarded bacon slicer.**

H. White

CLOCK THIS

A member of our local woodworkers guild came up with an ingenious device made from polycarbonate sheet for locating the figures on a clock face.

Members commented favourably on the idea until someone said, "why not use the hour hand?"

You simply fit the clock mechanism in place, hang the clock, and identify the vertical line from 12 to 6. Start with the hands at 12 o'clock or 6 o'clock, and rotate the minute hand through 360°. Mark the hour and repeat until the position of each hour has been marked.

It's commonsense of course – when it's explained to you.

N. Sheldrick

ACCURATE ANGLES

The mitre guide on my small table saw is marked in 5° increments, which is of little value when I want to make precisely angled cuts for assembling coopered or laminated blanks for turning. If the angle isn't accurate the ➤

glue lines will show it.

To set the mitre guide accurately, use a large protractor to lay out the desired angle on a piece of paper. The two lines of the angle should be at least 8", 200mm long.

Place one edge of a try square firmly against the saw blade, the other arm over one of the drawn lines on the paper. Then adjust the mitre guide in parallel with the other line on the paper.

You may find it easier if you fasten the paper to the saw table with masking tape. Of course the mitre guide should be extended with a long straight piece of wood, to give a good bearing area.

For safety the power should be disconnected from the saw while you are setting up.

Gary K. Himes

CENTRE FINDING

Finding the centre of square section timber is not difficult, just mark corner to corner. But round pieces are not so easy.

I have made up this jig from a few pieces of 12mm x 50mm, ½ x 2" timber to solve the problem. The jig must be made perfectly square and can be as large as you like to take the largest size possible on your lathe.

One piece of hardboard across the diagonal line is used as a marker. The other piece, positioned about 12mm, ½" away, is for support and rigidity of the frame.

A.R. Taylor

Centre finding jig

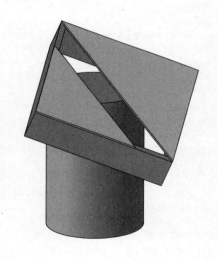

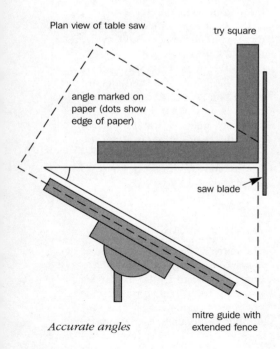

Plan view of table saw

try square

angle marked on paper (dots show edge of paper)

saw blade

Accurate angles

mitre guide with extended fence

28

FERRULE PUNCH

Ferrules cut from tubing can come adrift on homemade tool handles. To prevent this I've made a punch to indent the ferrule after it has been driven onto the handle.

Made of silver steel, hardened and tempered, the punch, passes through a mild steel ring that guides it and prevents the ferrule from distorting.

The ring of the punch should be made the same length as the ferrules on your tools and the hole for the punch drilled midway along the width of the ring.

This will ensure the punch is always at the mid-point on the ferrule when the ring is pressed against the handle.

Derek Pearce

Ferrule punch

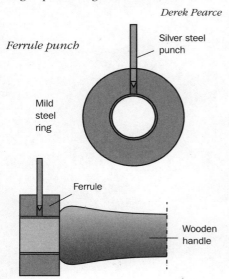

Silver steel punch

Mild steel ring

Ferrule

Wooden handle

SPANNER EXTENSION

The spanner supplied with my Clarke CWL6B lathe was so thin that it dug into my hands and was not long enough to reach under the lathe.

I made an extended handle from two pieces of 178 x 6mm, 7 x ¼" plywood, both recessed to accept the handle of the spanner, which was drilled top and bottom.

I placed the spanner between the two pieces of plywood and fixed it in place with two ⅜" No.6 countersunk woodscrews.

A third screw was added to the bottom of the new handle which was then sanded to shape to make it more comfortable to use.

I now have a spanner 280mm, 11" long, giving it more leverage and saving sore knuckles. This tip would also apply to any thin spanner.

George Capon

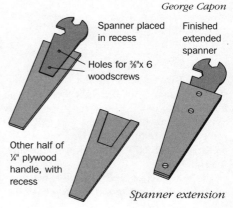

Spanner placed in recess

Finished extended spanner

Holes for ⅜"x 6 woodscrews

Other half of ¼" plywood handle, with recess

Spanner extension

Tough toolrest

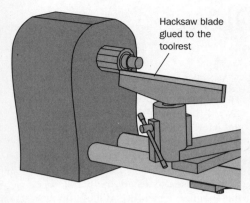

Hacksaw blade glued to the toolrest

TOUGH TOOLREST

As a novice woodturner I've suffered my fair share of dig-ins over the past few months and was not happy about the resulting dents and cuts in my toolrest being reproduced in my turnings.

Rather than file them out of my toolrest I decided to grind the teeth off a hacksaw blade and superglue it to the edge of the toolrest.

The blade has remained, undamaged, in place for some weeks now, with no apparent harm to my tools.

Geoff Jackson

THREAD CHASERS

Having difficulty in buying thread chasers, I made some from a high speed steel (HSS) tap with the right teeth per inch.

I ground away two flutes, then split the two remaining in half. One set of teeth was welded to a shank to make an internal chaser.

The other set of teeth have the wrong cutting angle for external thread chasing.

To rectify this I ground a radius on the underside of the shank, and in use I rock it to let it find its own cutting angle.

A better but more difficult way would be to fix the cutter to the shank at the correct angle then grind top and bottom faces to suit.

A. Nuttall

Thread chasers

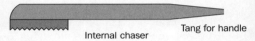

Internal chaser

Tang for handle

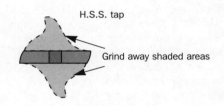

H.S.S. tap

Grind away shaded areas

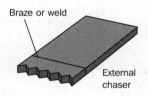

Braze or weld

External chaser

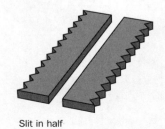

Slit in half

PINCH CHUCK GUARD

Jubilee clips on self-made wood pinch chucks are dangerous. Here's a simple plastic guard to protect your hands.

Cut a discarded 500ml washing-up liquid container (approx 65mm 2⅝" dia) to the full length of the pinch chuck.

The tapered neck of the container should be cut first, at the point where the opening will be the same diameter as the chuck end.

Then measure the length of the chuck and cut the container to the chuck's full length. Mark and cut a hole in line with the jubilee clip screw slot, and the correct size for a screwdriver.

Secure the guard to the chuck with a small wood screw.

John L. Elsey

A DEVICE FOR FREEING WORK FROM FACEPLATE

I own a Record CL024 x 12 and have difficulty in freeing larger diameter workpieces mounted on my 100mm, 4" faceplate from the thread on the headstock.

Hammering with the open-ended spanner and a rubber hammer usually did the trick, though it often only succeeded in springing open the spanner's jaws.

Then I had a brainwave – if the spanner handle was longer, so that it rested against the bed bars, and I turned the faceplate and workpiece anti-clockwise by hand, the faceplate would separate from the thread headstock quite easily. And it did!

A piece of 20mm, ¾" steel conduit did the trick, and I have had no problems since.

Peter Carragher

Ed: Placing a fibre washer on the spindle before you put the faceplate on will also help.

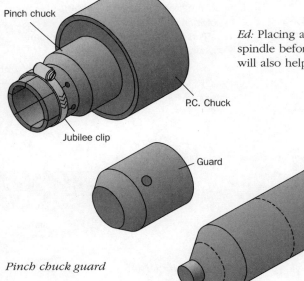

Pinch chuck

Jubilee clip

P.C. Chuck

Guard

500ml washing-up liquid container

Pinch chuck guard

31

INSIDE CONTOUR SANDING DEVICE

When sanding the insides of deep natural edged forms, I am sometimes painfully reminded how nature made wood a little harder than my knuckles. With this in mind I have made an 'inside contour sanding device'.

Cut 254mm, 10" off a garden hosepipe (you could cut longer lengths for deeper forms) and insert a small wine cork into one end. Then cut a stiff piece of wire 460mm, 18" long, bend it double and insert into the hose. Seal in with another cork at the other end.

Using sticky-backed Velcro, peel off the back of the hook side and stick it around the top of the hosepipe. Then stick 50mm, 2" foam-backed sanding discs around the top of your new tool, peeling the discs off and replacing when necessary.

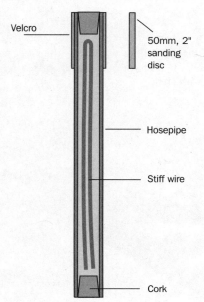

Inside contour sanding device

The tool can be bent to any shape and if it catches the natural edge of your work the soft pipe won't cause any damage.

Terry Hooley

SNAPPY DRESSER IS A SMOOTH OPERATOR

Having found that star wheel and devil stone dressers leave a rough finish to my grindstones, I now use a single diamond dresser mounted in a mild steel bar.

This is excellent, but it's difficult to keep it parallel and at right angles to the stones. I solved the problem by fixing a router cutter collar with a 10mm, ⅜" diameter internal bore to the steel bar.

These collars are used to hold shank-mounted bearings in position on router cutters, locking in place with a small Allen screw. The collar is positioned to run across the back edge of the toolrest, so the stone is trued parallel to the toolrest.

The results are good – but remember to wear eye protection.

Gavin Chapman

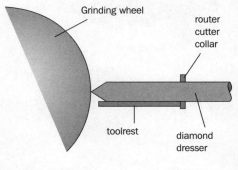

Snappy dresser is a smooth operator

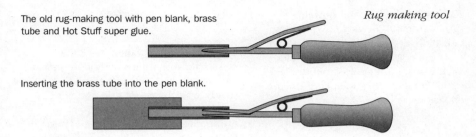

The old rug-making tool with pen blank, brass
tube and Hot Stuff super glue.

Rug making tool

Inserting the brass tube into the pen blank.

Rug-Making Tool Helps Gluing

I have found an old-style rug-making
tool to be useful when making pens, to
hold the brass tubes for insertion into
the wood blanks.

Slide the tube over the rug-making
tool, squeeze the side lever and you
have a good grip on the tube, which
can be an awkward component.

You can then clean the tube, apply
super glue, and slide the tube into the
wood blank. Once the tube is in place,
the rug-making tool can be withdrawn
by simply releasing the lever.

You should be able to find such a tool
at boot sales or antique fairs. A supplier
of rug-making material might even have
one.

Arthur Wilton

Make Your Own Simple Depth Gauges

The dimensions of these simple, home-
made depth gauges can be varied to suit
your needs. It's important they should
be accurate, so you no longer break
through the bottom of what would have
been a beautiful piece.

The gauge shown is made from scrap
timber, 305mm, 12" long by 19mm, ¾"
square. A 10mm, ⅜" diameter hole is
drilled, to take a piece of dowelling
305mm, 12" long.

A second hole is drilled 19mm, ¾" to
one side, in the opposite 90° plane, to
accept a 6mm diameter by 30mm, 1⅛"
long nickel roofing bolt, complete with
washer and wing nut.

The bandsaw cut in the drawing (if
you don't have a bandsaw use a fretsaw
or coping saw) provides the spring and

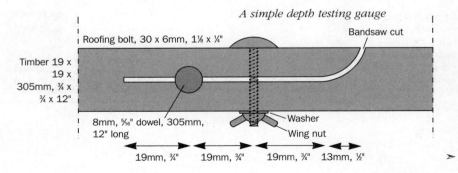

A simple depth testing gauge

Roofing bolt, 30 x 6mm, 1⅛ x ¼"

Bandsaw cut

Timber 19 x
19 x
305mm, ¾ x
¾ x 12"

8mm, ⁵⁄₁₆" dowel, 305mm,
12" long

Washer

Wing nut

19mm, ¾"　19mm, ¾"　19mm, ¾"　13mm, ½"

clamping method for the dowel.

You can mark the dowel with depth graduations if you wish. I have used a depth gauge stem from an old router, which is ideal in that it is round, black plastic and already graduated in metric dimensions.

Tony Evans

Tools Made from Scrap Planer Blades

I make my own tools from damaged planer blades bought from my timber merchant. They are made from high quality steel. I grind off the cutting edges and grind on a tang to fit the handle.

For draw knives, I heat the tangs each side and bend them nearly to a right angle before fitting the handles.

W.J. Gibson

Arm Support for the RS2000 System

Some time ago I bought the RS2000 system for turning inside hollow vessels and always had difficulty holding it steady with the pistol grip and side handle.

Enquiries at the West Midland and Heart of England clubs suggested that others had the same problem. Because the Stewart arm support is no longer available, I decided to try to make one.

The drawing shows how I made the support from plumbing items. I find it satisfactory for all sizes of internal turning.

It has an advantage over the original handle in that the hand grip is vertical, not sloping, which for me is more comfortable to use.

I wasn't sure it would be strong enough, but have found it is and that I don't get vibration. ➤

Handle for the hooker on the RS2000 system, made from plumbing fittings

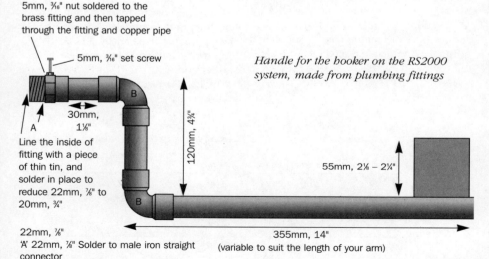

5mm, ³⁄₁₆" nut soldered to the brass fitting and then tapped through the fitting and copper pipe

5mm, ³⁄₁₆" set screw

B

30mm, 1⅛"

A

120mm, 4¾"

Line the inside of fitting with a piece of thin tin, and solder in place to reduce 22mm, ⅞" to 20mm, ¾"

B

55mm, 2⅛ – 2¼"

22mm, ⅞"
'A' 22mm, ⅞" Solder to male iron straight connector
'B' 22mm, ⅞" Elbows (solder type)
22mm, ⅞" Copper tube

355mm, 14"
(variable to suit the length of your arm)

Because the internal diameter of the plumbing 'through connector' (A) is 22mm, ⅞" and the RS2000 is 20mm, ¾" I lined the inside of the fitting with a piece of tin cut from a tin can.

Having cleaned the inside of the fitting and put flux in, I then soldered it in place. The aluminium arm rest is bent to shape and pop-riveted in place. The position can be varied to suit your arm length.

P.B. Sawyer

• See following letter relating to this tip.

STEWART ARMBRACE HANDLE STILL AVAILABLE

A tip from P.B. Sawyer described how to make an arm support for the Stewart RS2000 system, as he said the Stewart armbrace handle was no longer available.

I am happy to tell him that Dennis Stewart is still alive and well, and was the demonstrator at the last meeting of our woodturning club.

He no longer travels to demonstrate his tools, but still makes them at his home in north-west Oregon.

His armbrace handle, and most of his other tools, are available by mail order from: Craft Supplies USA, 1287 E. 1120 S, Provo, Utah, USA.

If you write to the above address you should get a free catalogue. The last advert I saw gave the price of the armbrace handle as US$89.95.

Howard Borer

MULTI-POINT DRIVE CENTRE

I've been using this multi-purpose drive centre for some time and have found it works well even with out-of-balance blanks.

To make it you will need five 50mm, 2" masonry nails and some scrap hardwood. Turn a piece of hardwood to fit your chuck and part off at a total length of 40mm, 1⅝".

While in the chuck, mark the centre and a circle with a 15–20mm, ⅝–¾" radius.

Make four diametrically opposite marks on the circle and drill five pilot holes for the nails. Counter-bore the centre hole 3mm, ⅛".

Put a touch of instant glue into both ends of each hole and drive in the nails. Punch the centre nail into the counter-bore.

You should now have five nail points projecting from the sharp end with the centre slightly proud of the rest. The back should be flush. You can set the radius of the circle of nails wider if needed.

P.R. Patrick

The multi-point drive centre

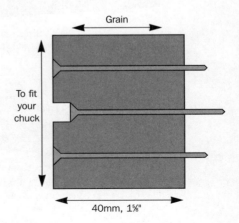

Grain

To fit your chuck

40mm, 1⅝"

Make Your Own Cone Centre

It's easy to make a simple wooden cone centre for your chuck, one which will take smaller pieces of timber than some bought cones, though it could be made larger if needed.

First, select a hard and durable wood, such as beech. Then turn it between centres until you have a taper that exactly fits the morse taper in the headstock spindle of your lathe.

Leave enough material on the thick end to turn the cone shaped recess. Trim the narrow end off the spindle and part off.

Insert the morse taper in the headstock spindle and turn the business end of the cone drive and shape with a conical recess. The size of the recess can be whatever size you choose.

A similar arrangement can easily be designed to fit the tailstock end, again to accommodate squares and rounds in the same way as the headstock cone drive.

A cone centre can be designed to fit a revolving centre with a removable point and hollow centre. This extends the advantages of the cone centre to both ends of the piece of work being turned.

A standard revolving centre could also be given a wooden, turned adaptor to make into a tailstock cone centre. You would have to devise a way to prevent the cone from dropping off each time a piece of work is removed from the lathe.

I have found the cone centre idea particularly useful when using small section timber. You should try it.

Chris Lindup

Make your own cone centre

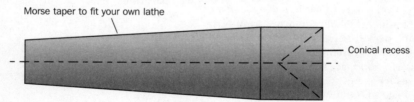

Morse taper to fit your own lathe

Conical recess

Insert the morse taper in the headstock spindle and turn the business end of the cone drive, and shape with a conical recess.

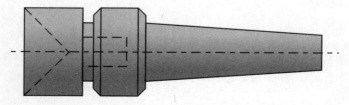

A cone centre can be designed to fit a revolving centre with a removable point and hollow centre

SECTION 5
TECHNIQUES

CLING FILM CONSERVES

When turning large hollow forms, or deep bowls, in elm burr or similar woods with areas of serious bark intrusion, turn the outside to completion and then wrap several layers of cling film around it.

You can now hollow the inside without fear of losing the bark intrusion, so averting the possible collapse of the piece.

Wrap the cling film around clockwise, to ensure there are no loose ends when turning. Simple, but effective.

Jim Botur

TURNING BLANKS MADE FROM GLUED OFFCUTS

One way of using up scraps or small sections of wood is to glue them together to make larger diameter blanks.

A maximum thickness of 32mm, 1¼" is practical, as the thicker the piece the more difficult it is to keep the joints square and accurate.

Make the blanks as follows. Cut the first piece 75mm, 3" square. Prepare enough timber for pieces 2 and 3 (see illustration). You will need about 1.5m, 5ft for this.

Cut the No.2 pieces slightly longer than needed and glue them to No.1. I used under-and-over sash cramps, but 'rubbed' joints would do. Let them dry overnight, saw off the excess wood and

plane or sand the edges square.

Follow the same procedure for pieces No.3, then glue pieces No.4, which are about 25mm, 1" wide, to the outer edges.

Bandsaw to about 305mm, 12" dia, ready for turning.

John Pedley

Turning blanks

How the blank is pieced together from offcuts.

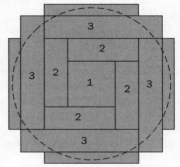

A platter used for a turntable on a 'lazy Susan' on which dried food is stored in coffee jars left in a kitchen cupboard.

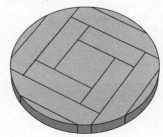

37

BUBBLE WRAP

There is always a danger, when parting off a finished workpiece, of the piece hitting the lathe bed or, worse, falling to the floor.

My solution for this is simple and cheap. Before parting off, wrap a length of bubble wrap around the workpiece and secure it with elastic bands.

The bubble wrap can be used time after time – providing you stop visitors from having fun popping the 'bubbles'.

D.R. Maunder

THREAD CUTTING

I would like to pass on a tip I learnt as a boy (I am now 72) which helps in making a true start when thread cutting by hand.

When using a tap or die, the lathe's tailstock can be moved away to start both tap and die by hand. My tip is, once the shank is to size for the die, or the hole size ready for tapping, use the tailstock to position the die or tap.

Put a drill chuck in the tailstock and hold the tap in this, then feed with the right hand on the tailstock wheel, using the left to turn the main chuck and the wood.

When using the die stock, place the die on the start of the shank with the arm of the die stock against a bed bar to stop it turning. Use the drill chuck in the tailstock to support the die as with the tap, feeding in the same way. This will give you a true start.

J.F. Skelton

PITH HARDENER

While turning a pithy elm burr blank, I had problems with the pithy parts which were very soft and came away like sawdust.

I applied several coats of Ronseal wood hardener – which is used to treat rotting wood – and when it had dried found the pith as hard as the rest of the part-turned bowl, thereby saving the costly blank and the time spent turning it.

W.J. Pimlett

WOOD HARDENER

I turn a fair number of bowls and, when cutting a dovetail recess for my four-jaw chuck, I sometimes find a soft or brittle patch of wood in the recess area, probably caused by fungi and spalting if the wood has been kept damp for some time.

This weak wood increases the possibility of the blank breaking free of the chuck during turning.

I solve this problem by treating the wood in the following way. First complete the recess, then lay the blank face down (recess up) on a flat surface. Pour danish oil into the recess to a depth of about 3mm, ⅛" and leave for two or three days to soak in and dry. Mount and finish turning the bowl, but do so at the lowest compatible speed, for safety's sake.

I have found that this method works with both danish oil and Liberon's finishing oil. I feel that it would probably work with any quality finishing oil containing hardeners and drying agents which would strengthen the wood.

With this method I can use the oil to finish the rest of the bowl as well. Products such as Ronseal wood hardener will probably be stronger, but will shrug off penetrating finishes.

Richard Pain

HOW TO MAKE A BLOCK PATTERN

A block of different woods can be cut in curved sections and used in making a segmented pattern ring for use in a bowl or vase. This creates a series of identical patterns used as a focal point in the main ring of the completed item.

Depending upon the number of repeating patterns wanted in the ring and the diameter of the bowl, the block can be of many different widths, lengths and heights. Use a compass and protractor and lay-out the curved lines before you do any shop work.

Also lay-out the pattern on paper before cutting or gluing any wood. Careful cutting, sanding and joining of the ends of the cut sections are a must. Any gaps will be filled with glue and will certainly show in the completed project.

For example, a 75mm, 3" wide x 125mm, 5" long block which is 25–50mm, 1" to 2" high can be made using different species and colours of thin wood.

The wood is glued-up (Titebond) and sanded in a step-wise level-by-level manner to create a multiple level sandwich effect with the face grain on the 75mm, 3" side.

The face grain or edge of the wood needs to be on the small side of the block as this becomes the curved section of the completed work and is cut by the lathe tools.

The top and bottom layers should be 6mm, ¼" thick to allow sanding and lathe work on the completed ring. This represents the bread. Inside, however, a variety of thin wood may be used to give a pattern, representing the sandwich filling.

When making this pattern block, it's best to use woods of sharp contrasting colour, as this makes the pattern easily seen from a distance. Each layer should be glued and tightly clamped to the bottom layer. Then each layer is sanded before continuing.

While this tip suggests building the pattern block up from the base, it's also possible to make a pattern starting from the centre and work towards the top and bottom.

Block pattern

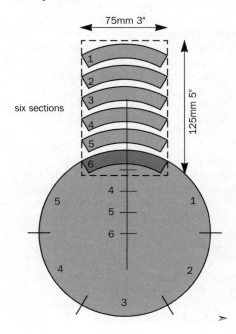

As shown, the six sections are marked on a block 75mm, 3" wide by 125mm, 5" long (viewed from the top). Each section is about 15mm, ⅝" wide, the six sections making a ring about 150mm, 6" dia.

The curved lines represent the outside and inside of each section and are marked with numbers 1 to 6. Some of the corresponding centres of the six circles are marked 4, 5 and 6. Section 6 represents one-sixth of the completed circle and is marked with diagonal lines.

A 200mm, 8" dia ring could consist of six or eight sections (patterns). For six sections the pattern block would be about 110mm, 4¼" x 165mm, 6½", with the rings being 20mm, ¾" wide when cut. For eight sections the block would be 75mm, 3" x 200mm, 8" with the rings being 20mm, ¾" wide.

Ideally, a bandsaw should be used; to separate the sections, cut between the two curving lines of two sections. However, a sabre saw could be used if the glued pattern block is not too thick.

For your safety, you may want to glue a piece of scrap wood on one end of the pattern block for clamping/ holding purposes when cutting.

Assemble three sections into a half-circle by placing each section directly over a half-circle marked on paper. Glue the bottom wood to paper. This allows for cutting/sanding of the section ends to the desired angle of 30°. (Note: six pieces means 12 angles times 30, which equals 360° of a circle.)

A second way is to use additional wood between each section, but this will increase the bowl's diameter. This way is often best, as the section is protected from excessive cutting and sanding needed for a good fit.

Complete the circle by sanding at the same time the four ends of the two half-circles until the fit is satisfactory. A table belt sander is very useful for this step.

Gary K Himes

CENTRING

Here is my quick and easy way to find the centre of square blanks, using a four-jaw chuck and a tailstock centre.

Put the tail centre in the headstock spindle with the chuck in position on the headstock as well. Adjust the chuck jaws to guide the wood on to the point and tap the wood to mark the centre.

S. Ashworth

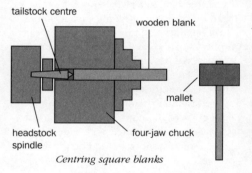

Centring square blanks

QUICK DIVIDER SETTING

Here's a quick way of setting dividers. I screwed an aluminium strip, about 100mm, 4" x 25mm, 1", to a shelf edge. With a centre punch I punched a mark near one end of the strip, then others, measured from the first mark, for every radius dimension I would need.

This simple device enables me to set my dividers in seconds for marking out chuck recesses. I have four different settings on the strip.

Neil Poston

MAGIC FORMULA FOR TURNING BALLS

My tip is an easy method of turning balls without a jig. It relies on the geometric ratio – one face of an octagon measures about 42% of the distance between two parallel faces (FIG 1).

For example, to turn a ball of 50mm, 2" diameter, first mount a block of wood in the lathe, about 90mm long and 57mm square, 3½" and 2¼". Turn the block down to a 50mm, 2" cylinder.

Next, calculate 42% of 50mm, 2", which is 21mm, ⁵³⁄₆₄" (¹³⁄₁₆" would be close enough). Turn a shoulder 3mm, ⅛" wide and of 21mm diameter on the tailstock end of the wood.

Then, 50mm, 2" towards the chuck, turn another 21mm diameter shoulder. The wood between the shoulders will be the ball.

Lightly mark the mid-point of the ball, then more heavily mark lines 10.5mm, just over ⅜", both sides of the mid-point. You now have 21mm shoulders both ends and a 21mm wide band marked (FIG 2).

Turn a chamfer between the lines and the shoulders. The faces of the finished chamfers should also be 21mm wide.

You can now mark the mid-point more clearly and the middle of the chamfers as well (FIG 3).

Round off the corners to create the ball. Sand and part off.

Henk Wolf

Three stages in ball making

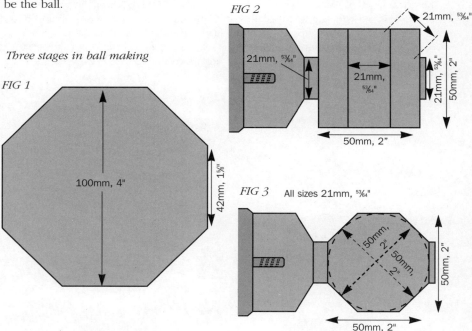

FIG 1

100mm, 4"

42mm, 1⅝"

FIG 2

21mm, ⁵³⁄₆₄"

21mm, ⁵³⁄₆₄"

21mm, ⁵³⁄₆₄"

21mm, ⁵³⁄₆₄"

50mm, 2"

50mm, 2"

FIG 3 All sizes 21mm, ⁵³⁄₆₄"

50mm, 2"

50mm, 2"

50mm, 2"

50mm, 2"

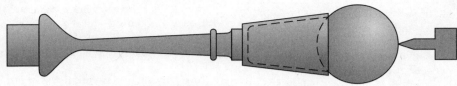

Brightly coloured hard rubber ball

USE A RUBBER BALL AS A BUNG

My most recent woodturning project was a set of three sherry glasses in beech. I had no problem making them, but did have trouble in making the bungs to support the piece.

I decided a perfect sphere was the answer, and my problem was answered when I saw a range of brightly coloured rubber balls in a pet shop.

The advantages of using a ball as a bung are: it is self-centring, it covers a wide range of diameters, grips the workpiece, absorbs vibration and can be taken in and out as you like.

R. Hartlebury

STOCK PREPARATION

Woodturning is my hobby, and sometimes I turn a one-off wooden knob for the electrical test equipment I use in my 'day job'.

To speed-up production of small components, and to avoid swapping from between centres to my three-jaw chuck, I use a hole saw to make a round spigot for the chuck.

A hole saw has a ring-shaped saw blade that fits over a twist drill and is used in drills for cutting large diameter holes. I set the central drill to protrude just beyond the saw teeth, so it does not penetrate the wood too far.

Stock preparation

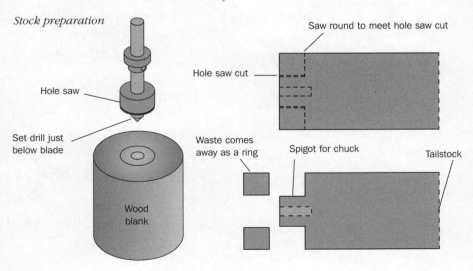

Hole saw

Set drill just below blade

Wood blank

Saw round to meet hole saw cut

Hole saw cut

Waste comes away as a ring

Spigot for chuck

Tailstock

42

I drill into the end of my wood with the hole saw and cut round the end until a ring of waste wood comes away, leaving a round spigot for the chuck.

Hole saws come in many sizes, but I find the 25mm, 1" and 32mm, 1¼" sizes most useful.

John Phillips

LONG HOLE BORING

When long hole boring, I hot-melt-glue a hardwood block to both ends of the work.

I drill a 20mm, ¾" hole sideways through both blocks and as you drill the longitudinal hole the wood dust is thrown clear, instead of blocking up the tailstock.

The holt-melt glue is easily removed with a hot knife.

The drill should still be removed from time to time to avoid overheating.

D. Gilbert

LONG HOLE CLEANING

To get a smooth inner surface on through holes in lamps etc, I use a valve guide cleaning brush from a Black & Decker de-carbonizing kit, mounted on an Axminster four-jaw chuck. This will also hold the piece for sanding and polishing.

The valve guide cleaning brush can be bought secondhand much more cheaply than shell auger or brad point pits, which need a chuck mounted in the tailstock.

C.R. Oakes

Long hole boring

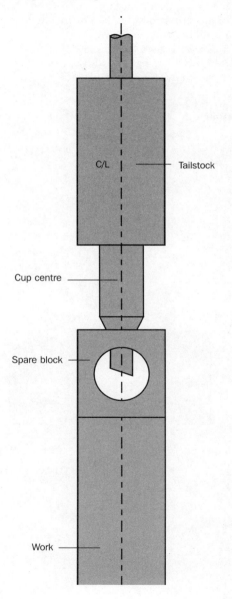

43

SHARP FINGERNAILS

I spent the first 20 years of my working life in engineering, sharpening all sorts of tools by hand. But, like many others, I still have trouble sharpening a fingernail gouge. I have developed a method of getting a good shape, without facets on the bevel.

First dress a radius on the grinding wheel, then set the rest to the desired angle. Hold the gouge flat on the rest, at right angles to the grinder spindle. As you grind, move the tip of the tool round the radius on the wheel keeping the shank at right angles.

'Hey presto', perfect angle and perfect shape.

D. Staplehurst

Sharpening fingernails

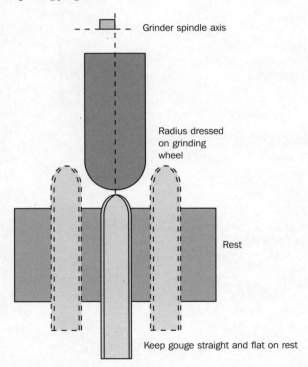

Grinder spindle axis

Radius dressed on grinding wheel

Rest

Keep gouge straight and flat on rest

SECTION 6
DUST EXTRACTION

PLASTIC TIPS

Plastic offcuts can be useful in the workshop, and I never throw away short pieces of plastic plumbing.

Short pieces of 75mm, 3" and 100mm, 4" dia rainwater pipe joined together by left-over 'T' pieces can extend the dust/shavings extractor duct system throughout the workshop.

A 'T' is placed strategically near each machine into which a flexible hose can be inserted. A series of removable 'stoppers' will, of course, have to be turned to block the unused outlets.

Useful tool racking can also be made from short ends of plastic waste pipe of 1" and 1½" dia, about 150mm, 6" long. I have several racks mounted on my workshop wall.

To make one, sandwich a row of tubes between two plywood offcuts with screws, then mount the unit on to a narrow shelf the same width as the sandwich. Tools placed in the upright tubes can easily be found and are unlikely to become damaged.

The tubes will collect some shavings and dust, but this will help support the tool and preserve that precious edge.

D.G. Grainger

Dust extractor from plastic offcuts

To dust extractor

Use outlet nearest machine in use

Rainwater pipe joined by plumbers' 'T' pieces can extend the dust extractor system throughout the workshop.

Short ends of plastic waste pipe are useful for storing tools.

Fixing screws through plywood sandwich

Tool rack

TOOL MOUNTING GANTRY

For years I have tried many methods of holding the dust extractor hose in position over the lathe. Bits of string, wire and even bungees suspended from the ceiling have all been employed, but now I think I've hit on the best solution yet and hope other woodturners will try it for themselves.

The illustration shows a mounting gantry which comprises two wooden arms screwed to and pivoting from the base of the lathe or from the mounting table. The two arms are joined by a length of ¾" dia dowel rod on which slide two mounting blocks fashioned from wood or MDF offcuts.

The dust extractor hose is fastened to these two blocks by means of a standard 4" plastic pipe clip obtainable from your builders' merchant. The type of clip shown is preferred so the hose can be readily unclipped and removed if required.

In use, the gantry can be swung forward towards the item being worked on and the hose in its holder is then slid along the dowel rod to the position where the part is being turned or sanded.

As well as holding the extractor hose in its optimum position, the swinging gantry can be used for a number of other functions. For example, a useful support platform for a measuring rod (or template) together with a sub-strip for holding a rule, can be made from strips of thin ply or MDF.

The platform is attached to the gantry by means of two further blocks, drilled and slotted to provide a friction fit on the dowel.

I find this a very useful addition when producing a number of similar spindles, being able to read diameters from the measuring rod and readily setting the callipers against the rule which is firmly fixed to its own little platform by

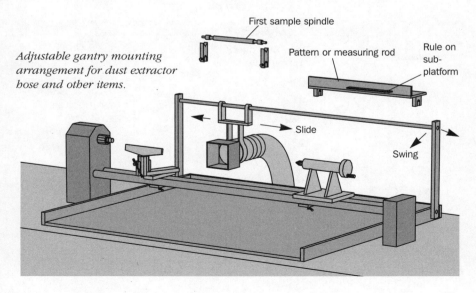

First sample spindle

Rule on sub-platform

Pattern or measuring rod

Adjustable gantry mounting arrangement for dust extractor hose and other items.

Slide

Swing

double-sided tape (no more scratching around the wood shavings to find that buried template or rule).

Another addition, useful when producing several similar items, is to provide two adjustable mounting blocks to support the first sample item. Again the two blocks are drilled and slotted to slide on the gantry's dowel and their uppermost ends are suitably notched with a V to support the sample.

The blocks are adjustable along the dowel to suit the length of the sample and locked lightly in position with a screw.

The blocks for both the measuring rod platform and the sample item are slotted so that they can easily be added or removed to give maximum travel for the dust extractor hose along the full length of the lathe bed.

G.A. Fradley

Shavings Removal from Hollow Form

To remove shavings from a hollow form while the lathe is still running I placed an offcut of an oval electrical mini conduit into the hollow, as close to vertical as possible, with the end touching the inside wall at about 11 o'clock.

The debris is pushed down the conduit, which is 16 x 10mm, ⅝ x ⅜" section by about 200mm, 8" long, and out of the vessel.

If the conduit is pushed against the inside wall of the form, the end deforms to that shape, making the removal of shavings even more efficient.

With this method, the particles are directed downwards rather than being showered in your face.

If the turning is deeper than it is wide, the end of the conduit can be angled on a mitre saw and placed inside the turning, with the cut end horizontal, against the inside surface of the rotating work.

James Symonds

An Easy Way to Clean-up Shavings

To minimise the chore of disposing of the shavings produced when bowl turning I suspend a bin liner along the front of my lathe. It's then easy to sweep the bulk of shavings into it, including those on the arms and front of my smock.

I roll one edge of the bin liner round a piece of scrap wood about 25mm, 1" square and 610mm, 24" long. With ➤

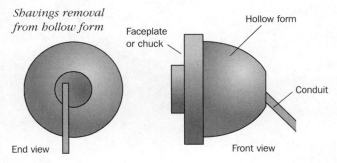

Shavings removal from hollow form

Faceplate or chuck

Hollow form

Conduit

End view

Front view

100mm, 4" G-clamps at each end I fix this to the front of the lathe table. The loose side of the bag can then be slipped over the ends of the clamp screws to hold it open.

Of course, any other system of getting a tight fit of the edge of the bag to the lathe table would be equally effective.

It's surprising how much the bag holds and how little it gets in the way. I use an old crumb brush to sweep the bench as this fits under my ML8 bed.

John Bleasdale

VACUUM CLEANING

To position the mouth of my dust extractor as close as possible to the workpiece, I use a window-cleaner's telescopic adjustable handle attached to a turned ball-and-socket joint.

By attaching a piece of cardboard, stiffened by wire, to the mouth of the extractor, I can catch dust that would normally escape.

Karl Decker

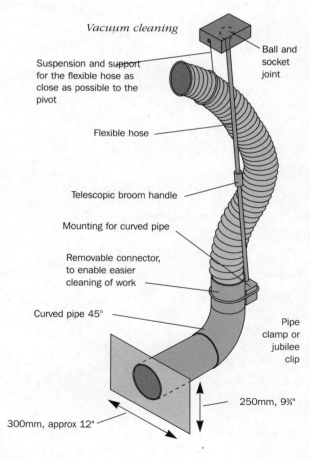

Vacuum cleaning

Suspension and support for the flexible hose as close as possible to the pivot

Ball and socket joint

Flexible hose

Telescopic broom handle

Mounting for curved pipe

Removable connector, to enable easier cleaning of work

Curved pipe 45°

Pipe clamp or jubilee clip

250mm, 9¾"

300mm, approx 12"

ONE EXTRACTOR FOR SEVERAL MACHINES

I have one dust extractor serving five machines. Each machine is connected to a distribution manifold with various lengths of plastic soil and rainwater pipe and old pieces of vacuum cleaner hose, the differences in diameter accommodated by turned wooden bushes.

The end of the 100mm, 4" flexible hose from the extractor has a square melamine faced chipboard plate fixed to it. This plate is a sliding fit under two rebated runners, which clamp it to the manifold base board.

The manifold consists of five pipes (or as many as you require) from the various machines, fixed into holes in the base board. A piece of carpet glued onto the board makes a snug seal for the sliding plate to minimise any loss of suction with the smooth melamine surface ensuring easy movement.

In use, the plate and its attached hose is simply slid backwards or forwards to cover the appropriate pipe for the particular machine in use.

Peter Symonds

Extractor manifold

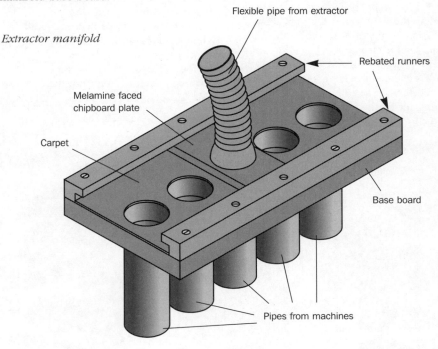

Flexible pipe from extractor

Rebated runners

Melamine faced chipboard plate

Carpet

Base board

Pipes from machines

DUST EXTRACTOR

I think some sort of dust extraction is a must, so I designed the following dust extractor and have found it to be efficient.

The front, sides, top and bottom are glued and screwed together with lots of glue to make the joints air tight. A 50mm, 2" hole is drilled in one side for emptying, and a tapered bung turned to a tight fit. For stability, an extra wide base panel of 6mm, ¼" plywood is screwed to the bottom of the box.

Three layers of cloth are stretched over the back of the box before the back panel is screwed into place. The cloth acts as the air filter and a gasket sealing the joint round the panel. The back is not glued in, so the cloth can be removed for cleaning.

The centre of the fan should be at the same height as the lathe axis, to position the air flow best. Otherwise, the size and shape of the unit are not critical.

Mine is made from materials at hand.

An old 150mm, 6" extractor fan is bolted over the hole in the front panel, to blow air and dust into the box. Other electric motors could be used, but the impeller housing must shroud the motor, and there must be no chance of electrical sparks igniting the dust in the box.

In use I found it to be a powerful and efficient dust extractor, which I move along the lathe bench to where it is needed.

R. Lord

VACUUM NOISE

I use my workshop vacuum cleaner for dust extraction on the bandsaw, and when sanding on the lathe, but the noise was intolerable.

I found that much of the high frequency sound came from the exhaust vent. This can be reduced by fitting a

Dust extractor

spare length of hose to the exhaust.

Spring clips attached to the wall near the machines hold the exhaust pipe up, where it doesn't blow dust around the floor or into my face.

Derek Andrews

VACUUM CLEANER DUST EXTRACTOR

The face masks I used to control dust in my garden shed, I found uncomfortable and fairly ineffective. But I couldn't afford (and didn't have room for) a ready-made extraction system.

The answer was to make my own. I bought a vacuum cleaner for £70, the type used in hotels and offices, with a 1,000 Watt motor and a large capacity for dust. I also bought a spare length of vacuum hose from a local stockist for £6.

The unit fitted easily under the bench, but I wanted to mount the extraction hose and head close to my lathe and yet be able to move and rapidly fix it in the best position.

I also wanted to keep the original hose and fittings unaltered, for general housekeeping in the shed. I solved this problem in the following way.

I turned a fitting to screw on the bench which would accept the original nozzle and the spare hose length. The hose was then hung from the shed roof over the lathe by a small spring.

I then turned several lengths of ball-ended spindles and removed half of the balls, creating, in effect, knuckle joints. The flats at the joints were at 90° to each other and were drilled to accept machine screws and wing nuts.

I turned another, boss-shaped fitting to screw on the bench at the back of the lathe. This had a central hole to accept an upright, tapered spindle also with a flattened ball end.

The upright spindle was locked by a bolt screwed through the side of the boss. I used an ordinary HSS tap to create a thread for the bolt, but a suitable bolt partly flattened with a file can achieve the same effect.

I assembled the knuckle joints with wing nuts and mounted a turned cylinder of hard oak on the final ball end with another machine screw.

This cylinder has a slight, internal taper at both ends to accept the free end of the spare hose at the upper end and the original vacuum fittings at the lower end.

This enables me to rapidly place extraction where it is needed most. In practice, the friction between the flat faces of the knuckle joints can be relied on to hold the hose-end in position without tightening or loosening wing nuts frequently.

All of the turned items I made from oak logs bought as fuel, but any hardwood would do.

When I need dust extraction over the lathe I can 'plug' in the original hose end to the boss, but when I need to clean the floor I can remove it and use the vacuum cleaner as originally intended.

The device works well and helps to keep the entire shed free of dust, something face masks can't do. You can adapt this idea to any size of vacuum cleaner – even a discarded domestic one.

I have enhanced the system by using portions of a plastic carbonated drinks bottle. The top end with the screw cut off makes a suitable cone-shaped hood to add to the oak cylinder. It's ➤

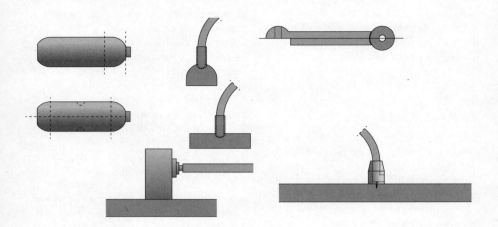

Clive Anderson's dust extraction system

transparent, lightweight, easily cut to size and can be cheaply replaced.

The hood widens the extraction area and is strong enough to stop most chips from flying around.

If the plastic bottle has both ends removed, it can be cut in two, lengthwise, to create a trough-shaped hood to serve the same purpose when turning spindles.

Clive Anderson

DUST EXTRACTION BUNG

I connected the standard 100mm, 4" outlet of my dust extractor to a 100mm, 4" soil pipe to distribute the suction around the workshop, so I could 'tap' into it for other machine outlets.

Having done this for my grinder/sander with a 38mm, 1½" sink pipe adaptor, I found each pipe outlet needed to be plugged when another was in use.

The 38mm, 1½" was no problem. I just turned a small bung. But the 100mm, 4" flexipipe needed a bit more thought.

I used one end of the large tin (180mm, 7" L x 100mm, 4" dia) which the wort for my beer-making comes in. It fitted perfectly.

I used one of those tin openers that takes off the rim as well as cutting one end, then cut out the other end with the old-fashioned type of tin opener that leaves the rim on.

With the beer kit comes a clip-on plastic lid, which clips on to the rim.

I push this tin into the flexipipe, so the end with the rim protrudes about 25mm, 1" and tape it in position with PVC insulation tape.

That's it. Use the wooden bung or the clip-on cap, depending on which end you want open.

Neil Poston

EFFECTIVE DUST COLLECTOR

I have found this home-made dust collector to be very effective. It's made from a cone of glossy card with a holed wooden bung (which distributes the air flow along the sides of the cone), taped to a rainwater pipe leading to a vacuum cleaner.

As the card is soft and flexible, it can be virtually wrapped round the bowl or the object being turned, and the bulk of the dust is sucked up. I can see how effective it is, because dust particles are not now apparent in light beams.

I used 50mm, 2" rainwater pipes with elbows, to give me the movement and location of the collector, and another wooden 'bung' to convert from 50mm, 2" to the diameter of the vacuum pipe.

The same principle could be applied to the larger 100mm, 4" pipes used on dust extractors and, once again, it enables the extraction to be close to the work without obstructing sanding, or cutting.

P.B. Sawyer

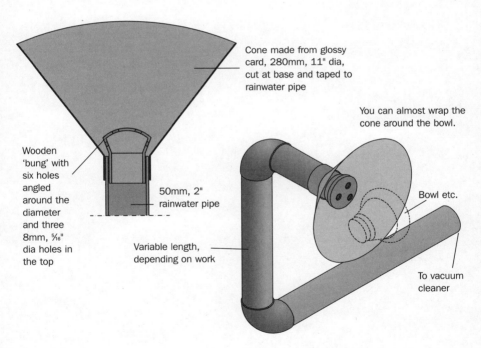

Cone made from glossy card, 280mm, 11" dia, cut at base and taped to rainwater pipe

You can almost wrap the cone around the bowl.

Wooden 'bung' with six holes angled around the diameter and three 8mm, ⁵⁄₁₆" dia holes in the top

50mm, 2" rainwater pipe

Variable length, depending on work

Bowl etc.

To vacuum cleaner

Home-made dust collector

Section 7
SAFETY AND PROTECTION

Safety Screen

An effective safety screen can be created by hanging a polycarbonate sheet over your working area by cords, supported by cup hooks.

When vertical, the bottom edge is about 100mm, 4" above and 150mm, 6" forward of the lathe centre.

The cords allow the sheet to be tilted and to stay balanced at any angle, even at 90° over your head, so that it's out of the way when you want to inspect or adjust the lathe.

The screen prevents shavings hitting the eyes and also most of the dust, though I still wear a dust mask. But it removes the need to wear eye protection.

The idea was inspired by the legal requirement to provide a safety screen to protect the public at demonstrations, where the onlookers remain clean while I am covered in shavings and dust.

"This screen is on the wrong side", I thought, and tried several methods of setting one up on my side, using adjustable timber framing, swivels, bolts and winged nuts. But they were all too complicated and difficult to remove or adjust.

Cords proved to be the answer – simple and effective. My screen has an extra cup-hook to allow it to be turned through 90° for use on faceplate work.

Note that the headstock guards have been removed for the photograph.

Tony Evans

Safety screen

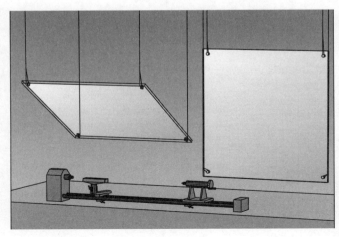

Two of my safety screens in place, the one on the right in the 'up' position and the one on the left 'down'.

DUST JACKETS

Here's a simple idea for keeping shavings, chips and sawdust off your clothes without buying an expensive smock.

I've found the ideal garment for turning is a plastic bin bag with slits cut for head and arms. This fits snugly round the neck, covers all your pockets and leaves your arms free. Shavings will not stick to it.

For best results use the thicker, shiny PVC type which cost about 10p, rather than the thin council-type dustbin liners.

If you want to go further up-market you can buy plastic dust covers with zips for long coats, dresses etc, 1400mm, 55" x 600mm, 24" for about 60p. These will keep your shoes covered too.

Smaller versions for suits or jackets measuring 900mm, 36" x 600mm, 24" can be bought for 50p in markets. These have thicker plastic and reinforced edges/seams, so will last longer.

Tony Evans

FIRE EXTINGUISHERS

Empty plastic washing-up liquid bottles, of preferably one litre size, re-filled with water, make quick to use fire extinguishers.

I have several positioned around the workshop, having had my share of workshop fires over the years, caused by steel wool behind the grindstone, and lathe shavings set ablaze when deep boring (I was in a hurry). I also have a wood burning stove and I smoke. There was even a deliberate arson attack by my wife with a lit newspaper: "I'll get you out of this workshop somehow".

Most workshops are ready-made

bonfires, with wood stacked all around, shavings and dust as kindling and flammable spirit based polishes. These plastic bottles are a good first line of defence. I find that just one litre of water will extinguish my stove and they can be used in pairs, one in each hand. A full one can even shoot upwards to the roof.

I know that they cannot be used on electrical fires, but I'm pleased I've had them handy on several occasions.

Tony Evans

STANDBY BATTERY FOR A RACAL AIRHOOD

The battery unit for the Racal airhood consists of three rechargeable AA type batteries connected in series to a standard male jackplug fitting.

Any woodturner who uses rechargeable 1.25 volt batteries in the home can quite easily make a standby battery for the airhood for a few pounds using battery holders and phone jacks bought from retailers who sell electronic components.

The drawing shows a four-in-line plastic battery holder with a dummy battery (consisting of a wooden dowel and sawn off 150mm, 6" nail) used instead of the fourth battery.

A female jackplug (phone jack) connected to the two wires coming from the holder provides the connection to the airhood once the proprietary battery unit has been removed for recharging. The standby battery can then be used while the standard one is being recharged.

The method of holding the standby is a matter of personal preference. It can be placed in a back pocket in the

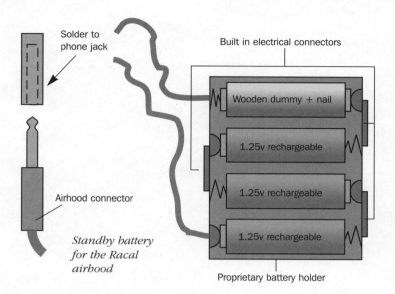

Solder to phone jack

Built in electrical connectors

Wooden dummy + nail

1.25v rechargeable

1.25v rechargeable

1.25v rechargeable

Airhood connector

Standby battery for the Racal airhood

Proprietary battery holder

turning smock after making sure that there are no trailing wires.

Alternatively, it could be attached to the front of the Racal airhood, in which case only a short length of wire would be needed.

Remember, when wiring up phone jacks, to make sure the polarity is correct.

T.D. Wright

CLEANING EYE GEAR

However careful you are when using sand/sealer and wax for polishing, you do get small blobs on your spectacles.

I've found that exposing them to the steam from an electric kettle for a few seconds and wiping off with tissues to be very effective. Repeat this a few times for the difficult ones. It does work!

Dr. N. DeNetto

VISOR PROTECTOR

Being an asthma sufferer, I find the Racal Airlite Respirator essential when woodturning. But I've found that the visor protectors – the replaceable plastic sheets – don't always adhere to the visor.

If the protector becomes unstuck from one side of the visor and 'flips' open, the fine dust in the atmosphere sticks to the exposed surface and makes it almost impossible to re-attach the protector.

Rather than buy new ones – since the old one is unscratched – I cut two strips of double sided tape and re-glue the old protector.

So far, the rejuvenated protectors remain stuck to the visor for longer than the original glue, without, I assume, prejudicing the respirator's safety standards.

C.B. Mather

SECTION 8
SANDING AND FINISHING

POLISHING STICK

When applying polish and wax to the workpiece in the lathe, I avoid the time-consuming job of cleaning a dirty brush by using felt glued to a wooden stick.

Only the end is used and when that is dirty it is cut off. It's a simple-to-make device which I've found to be effective.

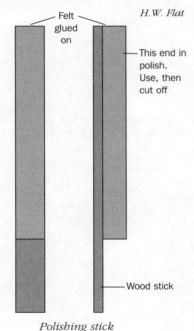

H.W. Flat

Felt glued on

This end in polish. Use, then cut off

Wood stick

Polishing stick

SAFER SANDING, WITH STYROFOAM

Sanding turnings which have soft, spalted or missing parts can be difficult, even hazardous. The rim of the turning,

if not continuous, will tend to be thinner at the edges after sanding. If there's a soft spot, it will usually leave an indentation.

Here's a way to eliminate the problem and save fingers from nasty, exposed edges.

Use styrofoam (expanded polystyrene in the UK) of about 38-50mm, 1½-2in thick and 150-200mm, 6-8in wide, which allows for both inside and outside, when you use the bandsaw to cut the radius of the turning to be sanded.

Round the edges of the styrofoam so that the sandpaper won't catch on the exposed edges. Place the sandpaper on the styrofoam and sand at a speed you are comfortable with.

I try to make the styrofoam a little longer than the missing part of the turning. Should the rim vibrate, when sanding inside, you may have to use

Safer sanding

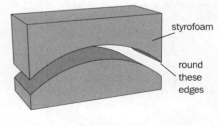

styrofoam

round these edges

➤

tape round the outside for support.

To support the inside, use styrofoam cut to the radius, and firmly tape it down.

Cloth-backed sanding belt abrasive will last longer than normal paper, and the longer length is easier to hold.

Sandy Dougal.

SANDER CLEANING

To clean any partially clogged sanding disc or belt sander, use a piece of plastic water pipe to grind it at about 45°, with the sander at full speed.

I use pieces of 20mm, ¾" white, plastic water pipe, of the kind used for cistern overflow pipes.

It cleans out the abrasive surface thoroughly in a few seconds. Any plastic water pipe is suitable and works like a charm.

Tony Evans

MAKE DISC-CHANGING CHILD'S PLAY

Self-adhesive sanding discs which have been in use for some time and need changing, can often be difficult to remove from the aluminium disc.

A solution to this problem is to buy the children's game whereby a woolly ball is caught on Velcro pads (I paid £1.99 for mine) and to strip off one of the pads.

This gives a 180mm, 7" Velcro disc in two half circles when the stitches and glue are removed which is quite easy.

The two half circles can be glued and butt jointed to a suitable faceplate or 180mm, 7" plywood disc, and sanding discs of different grits can then be bought, giving a quick change with no hassle. Wolfcraft sell 7" Velcro-backed

sanding discs in grits 50, 80 and 120.

And since you get two pads with the game, you can make two Velcro systems. This is much cheaper than buying a brand-name Velcro sanding system for up to £36, or small Velcro strips from a haberdashery.

Ron Pyrah

SANDING WITH SOLE

Smooth and economical pads which save your fingers from getting burnt and provide a good finish, can be made by gluing the latex side of shoe insoles (which cost about 50p) to abrasive paper.

Spread the glue – ordinary PVA wood adhesive is fine – on to the latex side of each insole and stick three of them to one standard sheet of sandpaper.

When dry, cut out the soles, saving the smaller pieces between each sole for rolling and sanding. Cut pieces from the soles as and when you need them.

D. Gledhill

Cheap sanding pads

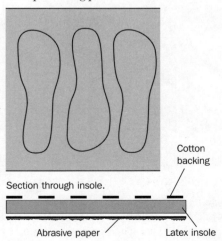

Section through insole.

Cotton backing

Abrasive paper

Latex insole

SECTION 9
STORAGE

HIGH HOSE

Don't throw away old pantihose. Tights are superb for drying out small, pre-turned billets. Just drop your billets in the legs, tie each one off and hang them high in your workshop. The rising hot air will dry them quickly and evenly, while each piece can be clearly seen for selection.

It also frees up valuable shelf space – and makes an interesting subject of conversation when fellow turners drop in.

O.B. Lacatte

BUD VASE FILLINGS

The discarded containers from denture cleaning tablets make ideal waterproof inserts for bud vases.

They usually have an outside diameter of about 16mm, ⅝" and can be cut to a length which ends just below the top of the vase.

I use a flat bit to drill a hole for a tight fit. Once in, it's almost impossible to extract them.

You can also use these containers for storing fret or scrollsaw blades.

Still on storage, empty plastic margarine containers (wiped, not washed) provide a rust-free receptacle for screws or nails.

Tom Lack

SIMPLE STORAGE

A few cheap magnets stuck to the workshop wall are useful for safekeeping easily-lost items such as spanners, drill bits and pins for pin chucks.

Also, a strip of Velcro from your local haberdasher is good for keeping Velcro-backed sanding discs out of the rubbish.

T.F. Holland

GARAGE STORAGE

Storing wood is always a problem in a garage workshop, especially long lengths. One solution is to dismantle old garden chairs and bolt or screw their U sections to the garage walls or beams.

Long lengths of wood or shelves can then be slotted through them, along the full length of the garage.

It's best to use coach bolts or heavy gauge wood screws, to avoid the danger of timber falling and reshaping your car roof.

Gordon Humby

HANDY TOOL CARRIER

A safe and convenient way of carrying tools – particularly woodturning or carving tools, to club meetings or learner classes, is to make up a case from 90mm –105mm, 3½"– 4½" plastic drainpipe and two end caps, obtained from a plumber or hardware store.

➤

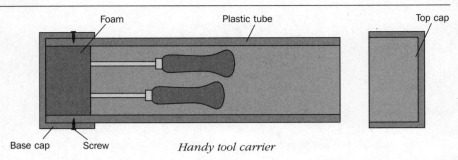

Foam   Plastic tube   Top cap

Base cap   Screw   *Handy tool carrier*

Cut the tube to the length of your tools, allowing for a piece of polystyrene foam block to protect the tips. This container will hold from four to six chisels.

The bottom cap can be held in place by two screws so that the foam base can be replaced when worn.

B.A. Hiley

TIDY SANDPAPERS

If you use abrasive paper rolls in your workshop, a good method to keep them tidy and easy to get at is as follows. Cut a length of brush shaft or turn a suitable length of dowel.

Slide the abrasive paper rolls onto this and hang it trapeze-like above your lathe using clothes line, wire or some other strong material.

When you need a piece of sandpaper, all you have to do is pull on the end of the roll and cut off as much as you want. No more searching under wood shavings for paper. Remember – a tidy shop is a safe shop.

R.A. Peterson

MIX CONTAINERS

Accurate measuring of small quantities of two-part plastic coating will often be

a matter of luck, but a polite enquiry at your local film-processing centre or photographic shop should enable you to obtain a number of useful plastic 35mm film cans free of charge.

These come in both black and translucent plastic with lids which snap into or over the open end, so some pairing up may be necessary.

Take a translucent film-can with a tight-fitting lid and mark on the side at 10mm and 17mm, ⅜" and ¹¹⁄₁₆" from the top edge, using a fine permanent marker.

Fill to the first mark with coating, then to the second with hardener, snap on the lid and shake to mix at a 4 to 1 ratio.

Label clearly, leave to settle and you have a ready-to-use mix which can be stored for future use if required, as the containers do not seem to be affected by the contents.

Do not leave the container on a highly polished antique dining table in full sun to prove me wrong.

Bill Gilson

BRUSH CLEANER

Black plastic 35mm film-cans are useful for cleaning brushes when part-filled with cellulose thinners. Do not discard after use but seal and re-use several times, completing brush cleaning with detergent and water.

The contents of the can will quickly lose its cleaning properties, but you will gain a small quantity of free, quick drying grain-sealer which can be applied before many finishes, including friction polish and wax.

Bill Gilson

BRUSH SAVER

If sanding sealant is kept in a tall jar, the brush can be left in when you put the lid on, so saving on cleaning and replacing brushes.

P.L. Billings

ABRASIVES HOLDER

Many turners now use cloth-backed abrasives and, like me, buy it by the metre. This often means there are dozens of small rolls of abrasive kicking about the shavings on the lathe bench. Come the time to sand, you waste time trying to identify grit sizes by touch, or reading the code on the cloth backing.

A few minutes making a holder keeps all your abrasives in one place, and if you write the grit grade on the outside they are easily identified.

My abrasives holder is made of toilet roll tubes and 4mm, ⁵⁄₃₂" plywood. I have drilled holes in the base to let dust and chippings fall straight through, while the abrasive cloth has enough spring to hold itself in the tubes.

Phillip Ling

Abrasives holder

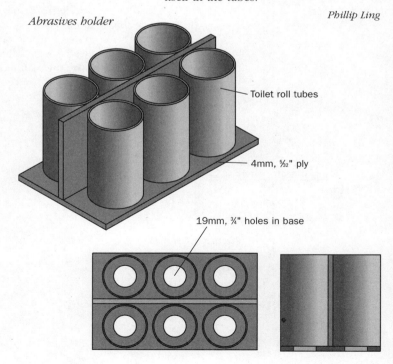

Toilet roll tubes

4mm, ⁵⁄₃₂" ply

19mm, ¾" holes in base

Airtight Seal

I wanted to fit a paint brush into the cap on my friction polish jar, but was stumped by the problem of getting an airtight seal between brush and cap.

Then I thought of an electrical stuffing gland. The 20mm, ¾" size I used closes comfortably around a brush handle diameter of between 10 to 12mm, ⅜ to ½".

I suggest you use a 20mm milled lock nut to go inside the cap. A heavy-duty lock nut will not prevent the cap being screwed back on the container.

Phillip Ling

*Cap-mounted
paint brush with
airtight seal*

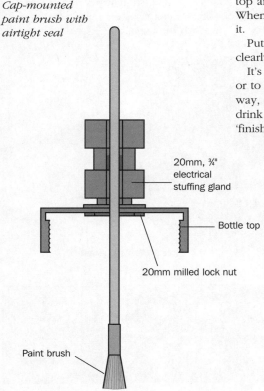

20mm, ¾"
electrical
stuffing gland

Bottle top

20mm milled lock nut

Paint brush

Use Wine Bladders for Storage

The empty bladder from a wine box can be used for storing woodfinish, as it excludes air and prevents the finish from going hard.

Once empty, remove the bladder from the wine box. Then, holding the bladder's spout in one hand, with a blunt instrument gently prise off the separate cap containing the tap.

You will now have a fairly big opening through which to rinse the bladder. Use a hair drier to quickly dry it. Pour in your woodfinish and replace the plastic cap.

Hold the bladder with the tap at the top and gently squeeze to expel air. When the liquid reaches the valve, close it.

Put the bladder back into the box and clearly mark the contents.

It's sensible to turn the box inside-out, or to obscure the wine labelling in some way, so that no-one can mistakenly drink it. Otherwise, you could give 'finishing' a whole new meaning.

Cliff Walsh

INDEX

A

abrasive cloths, storing 63

abrasive papers, storing 62

adhesives, two-part, storing in plastic film containers 62

Axminster Carlton Multichucks, making hot-melt glue chucks for 8

B

balls

rubber, used to support goblets 42

wooden, turning 41

between-centres work; swapping quickly to three-jaw chuck 42-3

billets, drying, stored in tights 61

bin bags, used as smocks 56

block patterns for bowls & vases, making 39-40

bobbin drives, made from socket spanner extension bars 7

bowls

making block patterns for 39-40

making jigs for cutting blanks for 24

brushes

fitting into cap of friction polish jars 64

polish- and wax-covered, avoiding the need to clean 59

bubble wrap, used to protect workpiece when parting off 38

bud vases, making waterproof inserts from denture tablet containers 61

burrs

pithy, hardening 38

turning, with clingfilm wrap to ensure integrity 37

C

car jacks, used to make lathes moveable 12-13

centre-finders, making 28

centres, making

cone 36

multipoint 35

centring 28, 40

ceramic tiles, overcoming problems of fitting to turned work 23

chainsaws, ratchet straps used to hold wood steady for 25

chairs, garden, used to store timber 61

Child Masterchucks, making lock brackets for 11-12

chucks

bobbin drives, making 7

collet, making 6-8

combination, making 6-7

faceplates, making 3-4, 22-3

hot-melt glue, making 8-9

lock brackets for, making 11-12

non-self-centring, making 9-10

pinch, guarding jubilee clips on 31

screwchucks, making 4

three-jaw, swapping quickly to between-centres work 42-3

Clarke CWL6B lathes

creating easier access to pulley housing 11

making extension handle for spanners 29

clingfilm, used to ensure integrity of burrs 37

clock faces, marking out 27

collet chucks, making

metal 7-8

wooden 6

combination chucks, making 6-7

cone centres, making 36

Coronet No.1 lathes
  modifying toolrest clamps 18
  reducing belt cover noise 19
cut-out switches for lathes, installing 16–17

D
danish oil, used to reinforce weak wood
  38–9
denture tablet containers
  used as inserts for bud vases 61
  used for storing fretsaw blades 61
depth gauges, making 33–4
dividers, setting quickly 40
division plates, making 13
dowels, making chucks to hold 6
draw knives, making from planer blades 34
drill bits, making jigs for aligning 21–2
drilling pen blanks, making jigs for 21
drills, electric, clamping in vice 25
drive centres, multipoint, making 35
dust extraction systems
  bungs for 52
  extended with rainwater pipe 45
  made from extractor fan 50
  made from vacuum cleaner 50
  reducing noise from 50–1
  with adjustable gantry mounting 46–7
  with cardboard dust collector 53
  with manifold for distribution to several
    machines 49
  with telescopic handle 48

E
endgrain, making a faceplate for mounting
  22–3
expanded polystyrene, used as sanding pads
  59–60

F
faceplates
  doubling as screwchucks, making 4
  freeing work from 31
  made from brass pipe fittings 3
  made to mount endgrain 22–3
ferrule punches, making 29

fingernail gouges, sharpening 44
fire extinguishers, made from washing-up
    liquid bottles 56
friction polish jars, fitting brushes into caps
    of 64

G
garden chairs, used to store timber 61
goblets, supported with rubber balls 42
gouges, fingernail, sharpening 44
grindstones, dressing 32

H
hacksaw blades, used to strengthen toolrest
    edges 30
hole saws, used for making spigots 42–3
holes, long
    avoiding dust clogging tailstock while
      boring 43
    obtaining clean inner surface to 43
hollow forms, removing shavings from 47
hot-melt glue chucks, making 8–9

I
indexing plates, making 26–7

J
jigs, making
    for cutting bowl blanks 24
    for drilling pen blanks 21
    to hold round timber without damage 25
jubilee clips, making guards for 31

L
lace bobbin drives, made from socket
    spanner extension bars 7
lathes
    creating easier access to pulley housing 11
    installing cut-out switches for 16–17
    making castor systems for 12
    making quick release levers for 15–16
    reducing noise and vibration from 14–15,
    19
Liberon finishing oil, used to reinforce weak
    wood 38–9

lock brackets for chucks, making 11–12
long holes
  avoiding dust clogging tailstock while
    boring 43
  obtaining clean inner surface to 43

M
magnets, used for storing spanners etc. 61
margarine containers, used to store screws
  & nails 61
multipoint drive centres, making 35
Myford ML8 lathes
  making a castor system for 12
  making a screwchuck/faceplate for 4
  making an adaptor for Graduate
    accessories 19

N
napkin rings, turned from offcuts 4–5

O
offcuts, glued together to make turning
  blanks 37

P
pantihose, used to store drying billets 61
parting off, using bubble wrap to protect
  workpiece when 38
pen blanks
  inserting brass tubes into 33
  making jigs for drilling 21
photographic film containers
  storing thinners in 62–3
  storing two-part adhesive in 62
pinch chucks, guarding jubilee clips on 31
planer blades, making tools from 34
plastic pipes
  used to make tool carriers 61
  used to make tool racks 45
polishing sticks, making 59
polish jars, fitting brushes into caps of 64
polystyrene, expanded, used as sanding
  pads 59–60
pulley housings, speeding access with
  Velcro 11

R
Racal airhoods
  resticking visor protectors 57
  standby batteries for 56–7
ratchet straps, used to hold wood for
  chainsawing 25
Record CLO24x12 lathes, freeing work from
  faceplate of 31
Record DML lathes, making quick release
  levers for 15–16
round timber
  finding centres of 28
  making jig to hold without damage 25
rubber balls, used to support goblets 42
rug-making tools, used to insert brass tubes
  into pen blanks 33

S
safety screen to keep shavings out of eyes,
  making 55
sanding, inside contours 32
sanding discs
  clogged, cleaning 60
  quick-changing with Velcro pads 60
sanding pads
  made from expanded polystyrene 59–60
  made from shoe insoles 60
sanding sealant, storing 63
sandpaper, storing 62
saw tables, angling accurately 27–8
screwchucks, doubling as faceplates,
  making 4
sharpening fingernail gouges 44
shavings
  cleaning up 46–7
  removing from hollow forms 46
shoe insoles, used as sanding pads 60
smocks, made from bin bags & suit covers
  56
socket spanner extension bars, converted to
  bobbin drives 7
spanners, making extended handles for 29
spectacles, removing sand/sealer & wax
  from 57
square timber, finding centres of 40

Stewart RS2000 lathes, making arm support
system for 34–5
styrofoam, used as sanding pads 59–60

T
thinners, storing in photographic film
containers 62–3
thread chasers, making 30
thread cutting, done accurately on the lathe
38
tights, used to store drying billets 61
tiles, ceramic, overcoming problems of
fitting to turned work 23
timber, storing 61
toolracks, made from plastic pipes 45
toolrests
modifying clamps of 18
strengthening edges of, with hacksaw
blades 30
tools
grinding roughly with electric drill 25
made from planer blades 34
making carriers for 61–2
two-part adhesives, storing in plastic film
containers 62
Tyme Avon lathes
making bottom fixing plate for toolrest,
tailstock & centre steady 18
making jig to align drills 22

V
Velcro
used for storing sanding discs 61
used to make quick-change sanding discs
60
used to speed access to lathe pulley
housings 11
vices, used to hold electric drills 25

W
washing-up liquid bottles, used as fire
extinguishers 56
wine boxes, used for storing woodfinish 64
wood
storing 61

weak, hardening 38–9
wood hardener, used to reinforce pithy
burrs 38

TITLES AVAILABLE FROM GMC PUBLICATIONS

BOOKS

WOODTURNING

Adventures in Woodturning	*David Springett*
Bert Marsh: Woodturner	*Bert Marsh*
Bill Jones' Notes from the Turning Shop	*Bill Jones*
Bill Jones' Further Notes from the Turning Shop	*Bill Jones*
Carving on Turning	*Chris Pye*
Colouring Techniques for Woodturners	*Jan Sanders*
Decorative Techniques for Woodturners	*Hilary Bowen*
Faceplate Turning: Features, Projects, Practice	*GMC Publications*
Green Woodwork	*Mike Abbott*
Illustrated Woodturning Techniques	*John Hunnex*
Keith Rowley's Woodturning Projects	*Keith Rowley*
Make Money from Woodturning	*Ann & Bob Phillips*
Multi-Centre Woodturning	*Ray Hopper*
Pleasure & Profit from Woodturning	*Reg Sherwin*
Practical Tips for Turners & Carvers	*GMC Publications*
Practical Tips for Woodturners	*GMC Publications*
Spindle Turning	*GMC Publications*
Turning Miniatures in Wood	*John Sainsbury*
Turning Wooden Toys	*Terry Lawrence*
Understanding Woodturning	*Ann & Bob Phillips*
Useful Woodturning Projects	*GMC Publications*
Woodturning: A Foundation Course	*Keith Rowley*
Woodturning Jewellery	*Hilary Bowen*
Woodturning Masterclass	*Tony Boase*
Woodturning: A Source Book of Shapes	*John Hunnex*
Woodturning Techniques	*GMC Publications*
Woodturning Wizardry	*David Springett*

WOODCARVING

The Art of the Woodcarver	*GMC Publications*
Carving Birds & Beasts	*GMC Publications*
Carving Realistic Birds	*David Tippey*
Carving on Turning	*Chris Pye*
Decorative Woodcarving	*Jeremy Williams*
Essential Woodcarving Techniques	*Dick Onians*
Lettercarving in Wood	*Chris Pye*
Practical Tips for Turners & Carvers	*GMC Publications*
Understanding Woodcarving	*GMC Publication*
Wildfowl Carving Volume 1	*Jim Pearce*
Wildfowl Carving Volume 2	*Jim Pearce*
The Woodcarvers	*GMC Publications*
Woodcarving: A Complete Course	*Ron Butterfield*
Woodcarving for Beginners: Projects, Techniques & Tools	*GMC Publications*
Woodcarving Tools, Materials & Equipment	*Chris Pye*

PLANS, PROJECTS, TOOLS & THE WORKSHOP

The Incredible Router	*Jeremy Broun*
Making & Modifying Woodworking Tools	*Jim Kingshott*
Sharpening: The Complete Guide	*Jim Kingshott*
Sharpening Pocket Reference Book	*Jim Kingshott*
The Workshop	*Jim Kingshott*

TOYS & MINIATURES

Designing & Making Wooden Toys	*Terry Kelly*
Fun to Make Wooden Toys & Games	*Jeff & Jennie Loader*
Making Wooden Toys & Games	*Jeff & Jennie Loader*
Making Board, Peg & Dice Games	*Jeff & Jennie Loader*
Making Little Boxes from Wood	*John Bennett*
Miniature Needlepoint Carpets	*Janet Granger*
Turning Miniatures in Wood	*John Sainsbury*
Turning Wooden Toys	*Terry Lawrence*

CREATIVE CRAFTS

Celtic Knotwork Designs	*Sheila Sturrock*
Collage from Seeds, Leaves and Flowers	*Joan Carver*
The Complete Pyrography	*Stephen Poole*
Creating Knitwear Designs	*Pat Ashforth & Steve Plummer*
Cross Stitch on Colour	*Sheena Rogers*
Embroidery Tips & Hints	*Harold Hayes*
Making Knitwear Fit	*Pat Ashforth & Steve Plummer*
Miniature Needlepoint Carpets	*Janet Granger*
Tatting Collage	*Lindsay Rogers*

UPHOLSTERY & FURNITURE

Care & Repair	*GMC Publications*
Complete Woodfinishing	*Ian Hosker*
Woodfinishing Handbook (Practical Crafts)	*Ian Hosker*
Furniture Projects	*Rod Wales*
Furniture Restoration (Practical Crafts)	*Kevin Jan Bonner*
Furniture Restoration & Repair for Beginners	*Kevin Jan Bonner*
Green Woodwork	*Mike Abbott*
Making Fine Furniture	*Tom Darby*
Making Shaker Furniture	*Barry Jackson*
Pine Furniture Projects	*Dave Mackenzie*
Seat Weaving (Practical Crafts)	*Ricky Holdstock*
Upholsterer's Pocket Reference Book	*David James*
Upholstery: A Complete Course	*David James*
Upholstery: Techniques & Projects	*David James*

DOLLS' HOUSES & DOLLS' HOUSE FURNITURE

Architecture for Dolls' Houses	*Joyce Percival*
A Beginners' Guide to the Dolls' House Hobby	*Jean Nisbett*
The Complete Dolls' House Book	*Jean Nisbett*
'Easy-to-Make Dolls' House Accessories	*Andrea Barham*
Make Your Own Dolls' House Furniture	*Maurice Harper*
Making Dolls' House Furniture	*Patricia King*
Making Period Dolls' House Accessories	*Andrea Barham*
Making Period Dolls' House Furniture	*Derek & Sheila Rowbottom*
Making Victorian Dolls' House Furniture	*Patricia King*
Miniature Needlepoint Carpets	*Janet Granger*
The Secrets of the Dolls' House Makers	*Jean Nisbett*

OTHER BOOKS

Guide to Marketing	*GMC Publications*
Woodworkers' Career & Educational Source Book	*GMC Publications*

VIDEOS

Carving a Figure: The Female Form	*Ray Gonzalez*
The Traditional Upholstery Workshop Part 1: *Drop-in & Pinstuffed Seats*	*David James*
The Traditional Upholstery Workshop Part 2: *Stuffover Upholstery*	*David James*
Hollow Turning	*John Jordan*
Bowl Turning	*John Jordan*
Sharpening Turning & Carving Tools	*Jim Kingshott*
Sharpening the Professional Way	*Jim Kingshott*
Woodturning: A Foundation Course	*Keith Rowley*
Elliptical Turning	*David Springett*
Woodturning Wizardry	*David Springett*
Turning Between Centres: The Basics	*Dennis White*
Turning Bowls	*Dennis White*
Boxes, Goblets & Screw Threads	*Dennis White*
Novelties & Projects	*Dennis White*
Classic Profiles	*Dennis White*
Twists & Advanced Turning	*Dennis White*

MAGAZINES

WOODCARVING	BUSINESSMATTERS
WOODTURNING	FURNITURE & CABINETMAKING
TOYMAKING	CREATIVE IDEAS FOR THE HOME

The above represents a full list of all titles currently published or scheduled to be published. All are available direct from the Publishers or through bookshops, newsagents and specialist retailers. To place an order, or to obtain a complete catalogue, contact:

GMC Publications, 166 High Street, Lewes, East Sussex BN7 1XU United Kingdom
Tel: 01273 488005 Fax: 01273 478606
Orders by credit card are accepted